HOW PARENTS CAN COUNSEL THEIR CHILDREN

FRIENDS, ALLIES, AND COUNSELORS OF CHILDREN

A talk in Ashford, Connecticut, USA
December 30, 1987

Co-Counseling started in the early 1950's. People soon got some idea that we had a tool that could really improve the way they lived their lives — not by an outside improvement but by an internal improvement. The people themselves got to improve the way their lives went. People became interested in using that with everyone they cared about and very quickly thought about using it with their children. So, people tried to use counseling with their children in the 1950's and '60's. They had some success, but it was very limited. We were doing battle with all of the rigidities that we have about children that came in on us as we were children; we were not yet able to think clearly enough as a group to be able to use counseling well with young ones.

In the early 1970's we finally had the right situation that we could actually look at counseling young ones and undertake it as a project. We had collected enough information and experience, and there occurred a concentration of parents of young children in one place. The work could actually begin. So, beginning in the early 1970's on through today, we have worked hard to collect information and to try out our hunches. We've tried to apply what we had learned with the 20 years of counseling that had gone on before, to use it with young people, especially the very young.

In the fifteen years since then we have used these ideas with children enough that we are now in a position to be confident. We know enough to make very substantial differences in the lives of children, of any child that we can bring the resource to. When we can collect a few adults who know some of what we've learned, that's enough to start making large changes in the lives of the children around, as substantial changes as we've been able to make in the lives of adults through these years.

BETTER OPPORTUNITIES

In some ways the changes are even more substantial because the opportunities we have with children are different, and better, in a sense, than the ones we have with each other as adults. We have a chance to reach human beings who have not yet accumulated all of the distresses that we're used to struggling through as adults; who have not forgotten what we have struggled to relearn under the name "Co-Counseling;" who have easier access to the channels of discharge, this healing process that lets us regain anything a distress incident appears to have taken away from us. (Of course, those incidents only *appear* to diminish us; they confuse us and leave us muddled enough that we can't remember what we are capable of.) This process brings back our clarity. It's possible to get it all back. Our children, by and large, have much smaller collections of these distresses to fight through, and their access to this process is much more immediate than ours.

We've come to fully realize how complete a human being is, how complete that intelligence is, long before they are born. The one confusion we struggled against a lot initially, and still struggle against, but slowly have become more clear on, is that a child is very different from the way society pictures her or him. A child is a complete and fully *intelligent* creature in the best sense of the human meaning of the word as we've defined it in Co-Counseling — able to be aware of the universe and come up with accurate, tailor-made responses to the universe, to that situation that they're in, without limit, immediately and without hesitation, and enjoy every bit of it. This capability is there long before we see them. They're collecting information and practicing that ability long before they get out to us.

The information may come through to them a little muffled until after birth. The extent to which they can use their bodies to practice motions may be a bit limited, but I know a number of mothers who, when watching their young ones stretch soon after birth, recognize the motions. They're very familiar motions; they've felt them for a long time and can see the similarities.

COMPLETE RESPECT

The young one is a full human being, and because of that, deserves complete respect. A child is a full human being who is in a very different place in his or her development than we as adults happen to be at this moment. Young ones are in a position where they need to practice and learn and acquire information at a tremendous rate.

It is hard for us to imagine how much information young ones are pulling in all the time, every single moment. Everything is new for awhile. Everything is fascinating. Information just piles in. That's one of the reasons for all the little naps that very young ones take. They've got to close off the new information for awhile, go to sleep and make sense of what they've already received, then come back out.

Our society has not given us that picture of young ones. Our society has conditioned us to think of them as cute and adorable and helpless. So we sympathize and cuddle, but we don't easily think about them as independent creatures; as having ideas of their own from the very beginning; as having wishes of their own; as making attempts to carry out those wishes right from the beginning. But, apparently we all did, and *all children do*!

We adults continually fall back on our projections about the child, even though we struggle against doing this: our projections of our feelings, of our understandings of the child. It's one of those big struggles we went through in learning how to use counseling for young ones. We erroneously expect such projections to be an adequate picture of what life is like for the young one. We must continually remind ourselves that this is a new, unique creature with a fully functional mind, with different information already than we have, with different wishes already than we've ever had, and that we have to respect that and nurture it and encourage it. We want each of our children to be a fully independent and unique creature, not like us in any way at all unless he or she chooses it. It must be entirely their choice. The ways that we have worked our lives out well may serve as a model temporarily for theirs: it's only temporarily, but the better you've figured out certain areas, the more useful you will be for them and the more they will be like you for awhile. Unless distresses get in there, all of that eventually, of course, disappears; they will become their own entirely unique creatures.

FULLY EXPECTANT

Unless she has picked up distresses before and during birth, a child comes out expecting to be fully human. Apparently we all expect other people to be out here with similar expectations, with similar hopes and high goals. We apparently expect to be able to get people to listen to us. Children expect others to understand the discharge process, to consider them as unique and fully human creatures and to be able to listen to them and help them work on things. Right from the beginning every child tries to make things work, makes valiant attempts for years and years and years with very little encouragement from us. They keep trying.

Children expect to be independent, to have their own lives. They expect us to understand that and be helpful. Children come out joyous — facing all the challenges, even the difficulties, with some sense of enjoyment and joyfulness of the challenge, some enjoyment about simply *being,* right from the beginning.

I think that is one of the slightly reactive reasons why a lot of us have children; we look for that reminder of what life *could* be like. We have a slight memory of having felt that way once and some hope that this little one will remind us of it enough that we want the little one around. I've known a number of people for whom that's been a major reason for having a lot of children. As soon as one child starts to lose it, it's time to get another so that there is a hint of that reality around the household. It's understandable. There are very few hints of that nature around us coming from anyone other than very small children. But it's not a good motivation from the child's point of view. They have a life of their own to follow, and if this is our main motivation, we're not going to be very understanding of that separate and developing life.

What children come out to, of course, is very different than that expectation. Children come out to us, and we're all right. In fact, we're rather good. Almost universally, we fight to put aside the pull of the damage we've suffered, for that child. We make a real attempt to be as human as we ever are with that child. We push as hard as we can to be there — to see the child, to be pleased with the child. People who have not managed to be pleased about much of anything for decades, open up and look alive and smile and want to be close to the child — want to be friendly to the child and wish the child well, even though they've not managed to wish anyone well for many years. We struggle to be as human as we possibly can for that youngster. That is a major accomplishment; that is quite something when you realize the struggles that we've all gone through. We're able to somehow push all that aside and try to be there.

OUR OWN CHILDHOODS

The difficulty, of course, is that we are pushing aside massive amounts of distress because no one was there when we arrived. No one was there who could consistently hold out the hopes and expectations and the resources to let us be fully human. We have built up this large accumulation; each one of us has our unique accumulation. Some of it is determined by groups we've belonged to. Great portions of it were delivered to us by our particular family, and they, of course, were just passing on things that they got. There was no intent on anyone's part to pass on any of the distresses or to inflict them on us, but they were passed on to us, so we're not able to remember to be out there with the young one consistently. We make real attempts, and it makes a difference when we make those attempts, but most young ones come out to a momentary hopefulness that gets covered over by restimulations and difficulties from the adults around. And so, though they may attempt to use this process and work free of the distresses, there seems never to be enough resource, never a clear enough picture of reality for them to refer to so that the process can go on well for very long.

For a young one to be able to use this process seems to require a reference point around him, perhaps because his picture of the universe is not well-formed yet. He has not had the chance to collect information. He has not had a chance to get the physical dexterity and muscle so that he can really sense himself as an independent creature. Perhaps because of that there is a need for a reference point — a need for a good picture of the universe for awhile while theirs is being constructed. The lack of that is very hard, very confusing to a young one, and most children never get a very good approximation of the reality around them to refer to. They come out and see us in our confusions and worries and upsets. I suspect for most children that's the predominant "noise" in their environment. Most of the time that is what is surrounding them.

REALITY BECOMES HIDDEN

Life is confused enough that people don't remember to try and give an accurate picture of the world to themselves or to their children a large part of the time. Because of this, the discharge process doesn't work well for children for long — because of a lack of encouragement, a lack of resource, a lack of support, a lack of respect for them as full creatures. The distresses start to pile in. The little hurts — from things like sharp points, hunger, the cold, and the temperature being too high — all of those distresses come in; also, the distresses of adults' unawareness, not just distresses we actively act out but the times we blank out while we try to be there. The young one sees this glazed-eyed creature there. I think it's scary for the young ones I work with. I've noticed something that happens very early for young ones — deciding not to look out. We've found that in a lot of the young one's sessions, they do not dare look out to see if there's resource; they go on faith, by reflection that someone is making approximately the right moves. They're too afraid to look and see if there's a warm or live face there.

Young ones give up on that awareness being there for them. We've seen this on all of us as adults as we learn to Co-Counsel — that we cannot look at each other and work. We work mainly by reflection. We look over there when our counselor is over here and hope that we somehow absorb enough, like two cushion billiards, that we get the reflection coming back to us. That's so much better than we've been able to have most of our lives that it works wonderfully well. Occasionally, we have sessions where somebody forcefully makes us look at them and notice that they're there, that they are trying to be there. Not without difficulty, and not perfectly, but they are trying to be there, and then things open up differently for us.

Life gets more and more cluttered for young ones. All of these distresses build up. All of the little individual distresses accumulate — all the difficulties, the mistakes they make in learning, all of the falls, scrapes, cuts, burns, touching things too hot, the distresses of the adults around them which get acted out. These distresses aren't always aimed at the young one, but she's witness to them. She's witness to the squabbles between her parents and all of the remnants of distresses from long ago that have gotten frozen in our society. The racism and sexism and everything else start being felt by her. As she ventures out of the house, she gets a view of the distresses being acted out by a wider and wider section around her; it's scary and no one explains it, no one talks about it, no one helps her out. So it gets passed on to her as it was passed on to us.

TWO POSSIBILITIES

There are two options, two categories, of counseling with young ones. One is taking our young ones where they are, having gone through this process of accumulating hurts. Another, if we're so lucky, is to catch the young ones before they've been subjected to this, before they've had to survive in this mixed environment. There are many things in common, but the work is different. If you get a clean shot — if you're there at the beginning — if you get a chance to put in a layer of the best picture of reality you have before the distreses get in there, I think it makes a difference.

One of the things we have learned is that every one of us needs a very sharp, clear picture of reality as often as we can find it. We need it to contradict things that we've picked up and that we're fighting against. The young ones need it as a foundation for their lives. One of the main parts of that picture of reality has to be that a young one belongs here and that her or his existence makes sense. Part of its making sense is that we are pleased with them, that we are joyous that they have arrived. We have looked forward to their coming with eagerness. We are pleased. Their existence makes our lives better and the lives of everyone else better. They are part of the universe; they belong here and will get to be here for a long, long time; they get to do whatever they want. They need to know that there are many, many of us who are pleased with their arrival, and that there will be a never-ending stream of allies, of people to cooperate with and enjoy and do things with and find out about. There's a large variety of people that they get to immerse themselves in. I think that has to be there from the beginning.

That has to be said every day, every hour; you want to communicate that in the best ways you can.

You never know when a young one understands your words. It is very clear that young ones understand your intent from the tone of your voice, from the expression on your face. As you get closer to talking about reality, something changes for a young one. Your reassurance makes a very big difference to them and their picture of the world and their willingness to go ahead and use the discharge process.

KEEP OFFERING REALITY

This picture of reality needs to be said to a young one — needs to be said to everyone you know — every day. We need to hear that every day. We need it because we're trying to reconstruct things. The new one needs it so they don't have to go through this process. That's one of our hopes, that we're going to short-circuit this passing on of distress and having to work back against it. We are fortunate enough to be a part of it. Very few people have ever had that chance before, but we want it not to be necessary at all.

The other main thing we need to try to do is to treat these new creatures with complete respect; to watch them and to know we don't understand; to try to learn what they are like; to not accept anything that has been given to us as we grew up or later about how a new human being is, but to try and learn it fresh. There are so many things to learn as you pay attention. Of course, one of the difficulties is that as you try to pay attention, you can't, or it feels like you can't. There will be a point, maybe in the first five minutes, or maybe only after three months, that your attention is pulled somewhere else. By and large, where your attention gets pulled is back to the inadequate treatment you had as a young one yourself.

YOUR OWN CHILDHOOD

The only way to really be able to pay attention to young ones consistently and with less and less effort on your part, is to go back and work on what happened to you as a young one. Until that is cleared up, being around young ones and trying to be different will consistently bring up your hard times and make it ever more difficult for you to pay attention. You're not powerless under that pull. You can still be there with the young one, but what you want at some point is to be free of that pull so that you can enjoy easily being with that young one for long periods of time, because it is a very enjoyable thing. The only way we know to do that is to go back and do that work — to try and remember what happened to us, to look at how we feel when we try to be around young ones.

If you decide that you want to be a counselor for a young one, what you need to do is to get contact with young ones. Go sit down at a playground and watch and remember. See what happens, see what the young ones do, see what their folks do, see what they do to each other — all the things. Notice the memories it stirs up, because it will bring up exactly the things you need to pay attention to if you're going to try to operate awarely in those environments.

If you're going to try to be a counselor for young ones who have been with us awhile and who have struggled with us, then the work is a little different in some ways.

I should say that the job of adults with young ones is not to give them perfect childhoods, not to make sure they never get hurt or they never accumulate distressess or that they always discharge on everything. That is really not our job. Our fears make us think that's the job. Our fears make us long for static perfection in some form. It does not exist. It is not part of reality and it is not part of the job of parents to provide this myth for our children.

I think a better picture of our job is to try to give young ones this picture of reality and to protect them from things they cannot handle yet, things that would do permanent damage, things they do not understand well — and to provide them the resource to continue using the discharge process as they gain independence.

FREEDOM, NOT PERFECTION

Our job is to keep them functional so that they can function on their own, not to keep them perfect and unblemished — that's not it. If you try to do that, your children will rebel very quickly. If you try to do a perfect job, your fears and rigidities will make their lives so dull that they will find ways to drive you up the wall very, very fast. I know very young ones who, as their parents come around them as they reach five and six feet high on the ladder, turn around and look at them and say, "no, no, no, no, no," even though they would crack their skull if they fell off that ladder. There is a real danger there, but it is more important to that young one to be able to stretch and try than to be hemmed in by the fears of their parents. I think that young one is correct. They have spotted a rigidity in their parents. This doesn't mean that the parents shouldn't do something to lessen the dangers. What it means is that their parents' fears have gotten in the way, and the young one is correct to challenge those and scare the daylights out of the parents until their parents work on it enough to figure out how a young one can experiment.

A young one is not asking to be in danger. Until the distresses get in the way, he's always asking to go as far as he can handle things. Our fears as adults and parents are such that we don't want to give them any piece of something until they can handle it all. That's our mistake, something we can figure out with a lot of work on our fears. Part of that is the fear we've inherited because we were not allowed to try. We can work that out so that our young ones can meet these challenges and go on.

If you're going to take on working with young ones who've had to struggle without people trying to be aware of them in the way that we know how to try to be aware, you face young ones who have given up on adults in certain ways. Not entirely. We all, in some sense, are in Co-Counseling because we didn't give up. We were able to hear that possibility because it was still alive in us. It wasn't manufactured outside of ourselves.

In some sense, no one gives up entirely ever, I think. Somewhere in there there's a glimmer of remembrance of a possibility that has gone on. But young ones get further and further away from remembering that. They get further and further away from being able to trust our stated good intentions to be there and make things happen. So the first task of trying to be a counselor for someone in that situation is very much like trying to build your first Co-Counseling relationship.

You try to build a permissive counseling relationship by putting resource at the client's disposal — at the child's disposal — and not expecting them to do anything in particular with it. You are pushing yourself to make yourself available — and your resources available — and offering that to someone so that they may try to use it.

DISCOMFORT OF OUR OWN RIGIDITIES

This is very hard for adults to do. You run smack into "adultism." You run smack into the feeling that you know what the child should do with the resource that you offer. The fact is you don't. That is just conditioning we suffer. The child will make use of it as they become sure of it, as they check it out and as they test us a little bit to see if it's a sincere and consistent attempt on our part or just a good idea that we lapse on very quickly. They've seen us come with good ideas and abandon them many times before.

For an adult trying to play this role, it is difficult and disappointing and restimulating because you have a wonderful idea for your child that will make her life better, and she won't use it. As near as you can tell, she's refusing it. She just wants to play instead of breaking into tears and sobs or shaking heavily and sweating from heavy terror. She wants to go play something; she wants to go play in the mud. She wants to do something we don't want to do, and here we're trying to make something happen and she's wasting the opportunity.

Of course what is happening is that we're getting the "adultism" restimulated that was pushed on us as we grew up and has seeped into every pore of us ever since. It takes over in that impatience to make a child do what we want. What we think is best gets acted out under the guise of counseling. This was one of the difficulties that happened in the early years of the 1950's and '60's as people tried to take this idea and save their families. We were not aware enough — we had not done the work yet to try and understand all of the things in the way.

There's a consistent difficulty in the way of adults being able to counsel young ones, and its general title is "adultism," or perhaps, more correctly, the oppression of young people. That's good enough as a general title. However, what you need to look at is what happened to you as *you* — what got acted out at you, and what you became aware of as you became an adult. You have to go back and look at that; not some general category, but your life and the way you collected the distresses.

What's happening for the young one, of course, is that they are trying to use your attention. Going out and playing in the mud, they are trying to use your attention. They are trying to use it to do something they have not been allowed to do, especially with you — play in the mud. They are making a very real attempt to go after things that they don't usually have a chance to go after. They are not going after their heaviest hurts because they're not safe to do that yet. But they're going after places that have gotten frozen — where there has been upset acted out at them. They're going to go try to play games and make fun and laugh about it.

They almost always pick a place—if you as parent try to do this with a young one—where they have a hard time because *you* have a hard time. That's how they happen to have a hard time there. So, you can expect to run right into a place that you don't want to run into, that you have avoided in your sessions. We, as parents, do not in general choose to talk about places where we can't stand our children. It is difficult to talk about those things even with our closest counselors—to admit that we don't want to do that with our children, to admit that we don't like our children when they do that, that we don't like dirty children *ever*.

Yet, that's the place we have to work if we want to be the resource for this child. All of the grimy little things that are hard to bring up in sessions are exactly what we have to do. It is, by and large, only when people decide to be that counselor for a young one that they are able to go back and work on those areas. It is really very useful for an adult to do that, and not just for the child's sake. I think most parents start out doing this for the child's sake so the child will have a better life. As it turns out, the parent's life will be immeasurably better for going back and doing that work, completely separate from the fact that it makes them a better counselor for young ones.

Their life gets better because they get a glimpse at all of the limitations that they function under unawarely at this point—all of the things that make their lives less active, less enjoyable, less close to other people; all of the things that have separated them as they became adults and that they have unawarely accepted as the way they should and have to be. Going back and looking at those for the child's sake lets you question them for yourself, lets you gain back large sections of your life and the flexibility of the way you function.

A LONG, GOOD PROCESS

It is a long process to look at that; we all have decades of being treated those ways and picking up those distresses, and they don't go away quickly. But, they start to shift from the first session; you get some idea that something is different. If you decide to do that work you know very soon that it's hard work, but you know it's correct. You see the benefits for you as well as for your young one; it starts to show very quickly.

Long-range, what happens if you continue to do this work is that you, as an adult, gain back large sections of your life, your choices about how you want to live, how you want to be with people, how you want to do things. And, for your young ones—the young ones around you, whether they be your children or just children you're going after—you become a resource. The children come to you, look at you, have some hope. The young ones are very quick in their judgment about whether someone has resource or not. We are all looking, checking to see if there is somebody around, all the time. The young ones are much quicker and less hesitant in their decisions. If you do this, you will have young ones around you. They will find you out. They will use you, they will climb on you and play with you and want to do things with you that will horrify their parents. It gives you certain challenges to figure out how to give some space to these young ones—how to get rid of their folks long enough so that things can happen.

The young ones' lives will change. Even if you do not yet get contact as often as you wish, it's very important that there is someone who comes back consistently every two months, every month, every three months, whatever; someone they can count on who, though you are adult, thinks about them and allows them to try things. There is someone who isn't upset; who doesn't require them to have a particular form in which they try things but respects them enough to let them be themselves and not have to shape themselves to be around that adult.

It makes a big difference that there's an adult who doesn't get upset when a young one dares to let a distress show, dares to let it bubble up and not have to pack it away and act the way another adult expects them to act, but can let it show; that this adult understands, understands it's a distress, *not* them; understands that they are not evil for acting out that distress; maybe cannot change it, but doesn't get upset about it, and at least part of the time is able to do something to let the young ones continue to work on it, to let the young ones make gains back from areas where they have gotten consistently trapped and more trapped as time has gone on. That hopefulness that there is such a creature in their lives makes a very big difference to the way a young one can look at life even though you don't have the chance to do major pieces of work. That keeps alive a hope and a possibility that's very important.

If you and the young one are lucky enough to have continued chances to be together in situations where there are not too many other distresses being acted out—people aren't requiring you to conform to some propriety or other—so that the young one has access to you, so that you have the chance to pay attention to him, say half an hour every week, things of major importance can happen for that young one. He gets more and more confident that the resource is there and will continue to be there, and he is willing to take what seem like chances to him to show you things and to attempt to work on things—to show you things he doesn't know how to work on. Then you will have some idea of how to assist, how to give him a push, how to provide the resistance. You provide a contradiction to how badly he feels about himself, which he shows by acting that badly with someone else; you're not upset that he did it. No one acts that way unless feeling just miserable about themselves. You show him that you don't get confused by that but go after him in his struggle with that distress.

DEEP TRUST, FRONTAL ASSAULT

They may turn and, if they're feeling very safe, do a frontal assault on you, either physically or just verbally. They may turn and look straight at you and say, "I don't like you; I never liked you." Just let you have it. It's like this double-barreled shotgun swinging around towards you. You feel the click of both barrels going off in your direction. If you've done enough work on your own distresses, it doesn't get to you. You understand that the young one is showing you how it feels and what's been done to them and you say, "Oh, but I love you and I want to be with you. Can't I be with you?" And they say "No." They continue showing you exactly how bad they're feeling, and you just stay there, warm and loving, and plead and beg to be allowed to continue in their presence. They will fume, blow up and show you everything; cry and stomp and do all the things they need to do that nobody will ever let them do. At the end of it they will come sit in your lap.

It is important to remember that young ones will show things that look horrible; we get restimulated and think those distresses are as heavy as ours, and they're not. A lot of the time the young ones understand what they're doing as they turn and aim that at you. They are trying to get you to be counselor; they're asking for assistance, often quite consciously.

The more you have an agreement on the session, the better it is. It is important that you don't let this little piece of "adultism" slip in— that you are the adult counselor so you don't need to communicate with the client; you just need to do the proper thing. It is always beneficial to the client to know that the counselor is thinking and not just trying to occupy a position—trying to look right and do right. The counselor is actually thinking well about them. This is very true of young ones. It is hard for us as adults to remember to communicate fully with young ones.

LET THEM PUSH

Even once the counseling has started, it is always perfectly all right to communicate, to talk to a child who is crying. You are trying to give enough attention to them so that they can continue to cry—to let them know that you understand what's going on. They need to push against you to work on heavy fears. It is very useful for people, children especially, to be able to push on someone as they work on their fears. You need to stay there and be with them to push against and not pull away or let them run away—not let the fear drive them away. Keep them nearby so that they can keep pushing on you. You need to tell them that's what you're doing because children are coerced so often in their lives. They're forced to do things, not by an aware decision, but blindly. Anytime you're trying to do things actively with your young one you must try to contradict that.

PERMISSIVE ONLY, UNTIL YOU LEARN

When you start out counseling, you have to be careful not to coerce young ones. Until you have experience with young ones, until you've tested your judgement, until you've counseled for a number of years, you need to not attempt to push. What you need to do is try to play the small and helpless role—to be down at the bottom. For example, when they're telling you that they hate you and don't want you around, plead and beg to stay with them. You're asking for their permission. You don't give up when they say "no." You don't go helpless—counselors should never give up the initiative—but you don't force them; you ask. The taking of that position of the small helpless one is a wonderful place to start because it is safe for the young one. It doesn't rob them of being in charge of the session, and it contradicts the pulls of adultism to try and force things to happen in session. It lets us, as adults, develop—it gives us a way to work and develop our perspective at the same time.

If you're able to continue this process and let the counseling go on, young ones will challenge virtually every distress they have.

FULL AND EQUAL

The relationships that develop between young ones and adults are full and equal relationships. They're not like most adult-child relationships we've had or seen. They're full and equal as two intelligent human beings at very different places in their lives; two intelligent creatures relating to each other, sharing information, sharing experiences, doing things together. The young one will provide a great deal of perspective and resource for the adults as these relationships form. Young ones do that. Young ones contribute to families very markedly by trying to keep the perspective for the family, trying to pull everyone else in the family out of the places they're stuck and draggy. Young ones hop into a room for a reason, partly to see if they can't wake us up. There are consistent efforts in those directions.

There is a very real contribution that young people give us that we have not easily been aware of. It is not an unequal relationship. We're in different places and doing different things and providing different things for each other, but it is not a one-way dependency. That, too, is a mistaken notion that's been foisted on us that we need to rid ourselves of as soon as we can. These relationships grow and develop and enrich families, apparently without end.

I guess the thing to say about young ones we have worked with is that they are noticeably different. They are confident about themselves and their place in the universe in a way that most adults are still struggling to acquire. They have a sense of themselves; they don't have to struggle to get it back. It was there at a very early age. I don't know how early is possible, but I suspect that it's very, very early. Most of us don't get it back until we've been out of the house for five or six years on our own and have figured out enough things that have contradicted the dependency feelings that we've had.

MARVELOUS FAMILIES

The families that have developed out of this are marvelous—they're all different. All of the young ones are different; they don't come out the same at all. There are certain things that you'd recognize, but they are very unique individuals—more unique than the other young ones around them because they are less afraid to be themselves. The families have that tone too. They are not like each other. Each is a very different organization and has very different relationships. They do everything differently, but there are certain similarities. They come out pleased with the family and communicating well and operating well together.

BETTER WORLD

I think this is possible generally for all of us who learn Co-Counseling well, and I think it's going to be possible for wider and wider circles of people much more quickly. I think this will make a major difference. A whole set of young ones—a few thousand maybe out of the next generation—will be able to come out without the difficulty and the struggles that we have to go through, will have a clear picture of reality early. I think they'll move a lot of processes in the world as quickly as we have longed for these processes to move.

HOW PARENTS CAN COUNSEL THEIR CHILDREN

A Gather-In for Parents and Allies
Seattle, Washington, USA
December 14, 1986

I think this was billed as an evening on working with children. Hopefully we'll have lots of time for questions. There are a few things I want to begin talking about so we don't just fly in cold.

We've just finished a family workshop. We were trying to figure out when I first started doing family workshops — it was about fourteen years ago. We've done various combinations of us, and now there are quite a few of us who do them around the world. We've done probably 400 of these, and I know I've done more than 250 of them. They're very interesting workshops if you've never been to one. Whether or not you have a lot of contact with young people at the moment, you would find them interesting to go to and different from other workshops, and probably very useful once you've recovered from them.

They can be somewhat of a shock because they're structured to allow the young ones to run things the way they want, to have the upper hand, and that means the adults don't. It's a very awkward position for adults to have to follow the lead of young people. This weekend we had seven-year-olds and younger, and what seven-year-olds and youngers want to do is generally not what the adults arrive wanting to do. Eventually the adults learn to enjoy it, but it's a shock at the beginning.

It's a re-awakening of things that were taken away from us long ago and that we'd forgotten we've even missed. It's also very useful in many other ways—in your perspective on life and your perspective about counseling. You can see what counseling can do for a small child who hasn't accumulated decades of restimulation on any particular distress.

For example, there was one very nice session this weekend with a little one. It ran about an hour and a half. Before that, he was wandering around clinging to his mother and looking at the floor a lot, just not able to make contact. After the session he was out in the middle, walking around and looking at people, sitting down next to them to see what they could do. You will just see changes that quickly.

It's very nice to see. It reminds us of the power we all actually have to make important changes in the world and in the people around us. We adults working with each other can get confused by all the restimulation, the noises we make and the sounds of struggle when we lose perspective and feel so bad about things that aren't actually that bad. It's nice to have this little antidote available occasionally.

If you get the chance I dare you to go to these workshops occasionally. We are somewhat careful about who shows up. There's a balance of one-third young people, one-third their parents, and one-third adults not their parents, who often play the role of cannon fodder for the workshops, taking the brunt of the play for a while until everyone can loosen up and start enjoying it. But those positions are available and they're worth it. They're easily worth it.

It's a lovely area of counseling, using counseling with young ones. Its benefits are so quickly evident that you don't get as confused as you can get in working with adults. You're not slugging away at the same thing that doesn't seem to move, and their feeling about that distress and the way they act in that area doesn't stay the same as you bludgeon it week after week with them. Things shift more quickly.

THE WAY IT BEGAN

The idea of using counseling with young ones came about fifteen years ago, and it happened around me. It's sort of an accident that I'm in this role of being the one that initiated a lot of these things and carried it on. We just accidentally had a great many parents of young children in my fundamentals classes all at once, and they dominated all the question times, and all of the questions aimed in that direction. So in some sense to protect the fundamentals classes, to keep from driving out everyone who wasn't a parent of young children, we set up something else for the parents to get started.

We've learned a lot over the years. In many ways it's exactly the same as everything else we know about counseling. It just has this added little complication to it: that we are adults and that we came through childhood and we picked up a lot of distresses along the way that we don't always notice until we're around children. The children, of course, notice them long before we notice them because we're acting them out unawarely for a while. We're doing the best thing we can, which is the best thing that our folks could figure out to help us along the way, and it's just gotten encrusted with the distresses.

PERMISSIVE COUNSELING AT FIRST

This extra complication makes things quite interesting and challenging. The role we've found that we have to suggest very strongly to adults starting to use counseling with young ones is that you have to be a permissive counselor initially and you have to work on your childhood. If you can be a permissive counselor and hang around the young ones enough (which really means following their lead and doing what they want), what will happen is that you will be reminded of a lot of things in your childhood that it hadn't occurred to you to work on yet.

Like anything you struggle with in your life, or anything you think to work on in counseling, the way you work on it best is by challenging it in practice, by trying to make it work and then going and getting sessions on it. It's much clearer where you need to work after you've faced the challenge of trying to do something in present time rather than just suffering it in a session and working on it there.

When you've taken on this challenge to be a permissive counselor, the young one will take you through all sorts of things that you will have forgotten from your childhood but that will start ringing little bells back there. That's the first benefit for us; that we go work on those things because we're pushed by our attempts in present time. In some ways we work on it to be a better counselor for young people, but the benefit for you is very quick, very immediate. Your counseling benefits you just as much as it's going to benefit that young person you're trying to work with.

You have to be permissive for quite a while, while this work gets done, simply because we get confused easily until that counseling is taken care of. There are so many rules that pop out of your mouth without any conscious thought on your part, and if you listen you hear your teacher's or your parents' or your Sunday school teacher's tone and words flying around the room, and there's no one else they could have come from but you! And you didn't really mean that, you didn't think of it, it just came out. To be a permissive counselor puts in a little block, makes you stumble first before you can get your mouth open. Often that's enough time for you to consider what was trying to come out of your mouth that you can stop it and you can just follow along.

The other thing that happens in these permissive sessions is that the young one chooses things that you don't like and wants you to do them with them. Parents feel like the children do this on purpose: the children study their parents, find their weak spots and present them to them. I don't think that's the case. I can understand them feeling that way at those moments. There is a tendency to head for those spots because our children live with us all the time, and our rigidities, our limitations are limitations that they have to live under every day of their lives. If you make a commitment to trying to go past those limitations, some of the most interesting places for them to go are exactly the places those limitations have stopped them. So they are going to edge out in those areas. Here, too, it helps bring up all sorts of areas it had escaped your conscious awareness to work on, and you can go and have very fruitful sessions right after having these times with young ones, and things start to shift.

You know as you discover occluded areas, things you hadn't considered or thought about or remembered, and start getting a session or two on them, your picture of yourself in the world starts to shift a little. Options open up for yourself. It's another very quick and real benefit.

I want to draw a distinction between what we mean by permissive counseling in sessions, especially with young ones, and permissive child-raising, which was a well-meant, I think, reaction to being raised authoritarian style for a lot of us in my generation, and just to try to keep that from being passed on, we flipped to the other side.

But there's a problem with that in that it really doesn't leave us thinking about our children. And as a counselor, no matter what role you're playing, you have to be thinking, whether you're following along and following their lead or taking a more active role; none of that is passive. A permissive counselor is not a passive counselor, is not an unaware counselor. You need to be thinking all the time, watching what happens, trying to figure out where it came from and what you can do to keep it going. It can be very enjoyable and challenging to be a permissive counselor; you are thinking about them and holding a separate, an independent, perspective on what is happening.

There are times, sometimes much sooner than you would like, where the young one will push the session past where being a permissive counselor is enough. Whether it's the first or the tenth or the fortieth one, the young one gets enough confidence in you that he or she will try to work on something where they need more than you following them along. And if you haven't been thinking about them until then, if you haven't been actively watching them and keeping track and figuring what's happening as best you can, it's a very large jump at that point to try to put it all together and be something other than the follower.

AN UNDERSTANDING OPPOSITION

The most common one that I think happens in every family I've ever heard of, in or outside counseling, is that the young one will try to get someone to do battle against, will try to find some understanding opposition, try to find a counselor that they can work on their disappointment with. And, of course, to work on those disappointments they have to get you to say "no."

We've had a lot of different experiences with this. We've watched families who have tried to be thoughtful and good and sympathetic to their children and give them everything they ask for; we've watched the child figure out how big they have to ask before the family has to say "no." They just up the ante week by week by week until finally it dawns on their parents that it's probably not correct for their twelve-year-old to be wanting a Cadillac right now.

That may sound extreme. It's not terribly different from what we've heard. Parents who haven't thought about this need, this need for a place for a young one to work on disappointment, try to satisfy the demands for a long, long time before it suddenly clicks with them (and sometimes it takes that extreme a demand to do it).

Then finally, when they say, "No, you know that really doesn't make sense," the young one can show all the disappointment they've been carrying for a thousand different things and work on it. They can work on it steadily and be bitterly disappointed and think of all the reasons why they should have a Cadillac; the sessions go on well until it finally resolves. Until then life is miserable because the folks can't quite figure out what's happening, and they're always trying to either appease or find some way to distract them with something else.

All of these things, and a great many more things, work in counseling with young ones just like they work in counseling with anyone. I've used all these things with adults—almost everyone I counsel with. They're almost always the same ideas. Your application of them is what changes, and that special complication of ours—carrying all of these distresses from our childhood—makes us have to work harder to put them into practice clearly.

CARE THEY EXIST

There are some other things that are very standard in working with young ones and adults. It's just easier in some ways to talk about it with the young ones initially. One is, that no one I've ever met feels very confident about their existence; they're not sure why they're here or that anyone cares that they're here, or that there's some value, that it makes sense to be here. You know how often you wake up in the middle of the night and ponder that question, or in the morning when you can't figure out why to get out of bed, or whenever it happens to grab on to you.

I think each one of us needs to know from somebody around us that they care we exist, and it's true of our children. We start out telling them while we hold them, while they can't walk, while they're ours in this way and dependent on us; we as parents and other adults feel safe enough to tell them how dear they are and how much we've looked forward to their coming and what a great joy they are in our life and what perfect sense it makes that they're here. Once they start moving off on their own it gets harder for us to do that. And I think we need to do that. When we do, I see children just blossom.

At this workshop there were a couple of them. It happens more quickly and harsher for little boys than it does for little girls. Little boys are supposed to march off independently, you know, and be little men, which essentially means have nothing faze them and be able to figure out everything that ever comes down the pipe whether they've ever seen it or not. They have to handle everything immediately, which is a tough position for a little four-year-old to march off into, but we do. This is not an extreme characterization of it at all.

This weekend there was a little one who had his chest out and everything, had the position correct; what was necessary was for me to tackle him and cuddle him and nuzzle him and just tell him that I liked him and I wanted him to be with me and I wasn't going to let him go away because I wanted him to be close to me. He would laugh and laugh and laugh and laugh. If some distraction happened, another young one coming in that I had to handle for a moment, other people who were watching would say he'd sort of sit over at the side and try to figure out how to come back in. He couldn't quite figure it out for himself. (Just like we usually can't figure it out for ourselves.) But he was waiting for the idea to hit my mind again, for me to stop being distracted from what I was trying to do and come back and try it again.

This sort of reassurance, as well as the physical contact—the physical contact is a very important part of it—is something that we, because we've been able to work with young ones, have been able to remember, and get to use a lot. It's just as true of you. That reassurance that somebody knows you and cares about you, is pleased with your existence and understands it makes sense that you're here, and likes to hold you in their arms, likes your very physical existence, is something all of us could use a reminder of very often.

It would be nice to make a deal with someone, even if they don't understand, just some little reminder of it. I did something like this in graduate school (which, if you remember school, is not the time when you feel great about yourself or feel close and connected usually;

you're in there struggling, trying to get through this thing). There was a secretary who had been in the department for forty years and we just made a deal. I don't know the basis on which she agreed to do it. I have no idea, but I would pal around with her a little so she was relaxed about it. We just agreed every time we would pass each other in the hall we would throw our arms around each other, twirl around three times and go on our way. It was real nice. It shook up the department a little too. Just some little bit of contact. Just a reminder that there's somebody out there that liked me well enough they could put their arms around me. That's enough. It didn't have to be anything more than that. That's a big reminder about a lot of things.

Working with children you get a chance to discover that. It's a little easier for adults to remember and to try those things out with a small one. Somehow society isn't going to step on you quite so hard if they catch you doing it as if they see you trying to do that with other adults. Their awkwardness is not the same. So it's a very, very nice opportunity to reacquaint yourself with other things that you can carry on up through the ages, through to your older friends as you struggle with these things.

That's enough of an introduction, I think. There are a lot of people working now, more and more. We've reached the point where people have begun to understand how important it is, how important getting this work done in families and with the very young ones is.

We got started a long time ago. We started a little school, which doesn't exist any longer. All of those children are near high school age now. They were two, three and four at the time. And, just as a quick report, I can tell you those young people are significantly different. They're really quite different from the way we were in many ways: the relationships they have with each other; how relaxed they are; how much they can be with each other and listen to each other (they can pay attention to each other for long periods of time, longer and longer); the way they are with the adults they know—there are teenage boys that will hang on and lean on each other. That they can be that comfortable, have that good a relationship, looks real good. They're also very smart; they are *very* smart. I have no idea what they'll become. They're starting to scatter and go out and do things. They're not at all the same as one another. They're very different creatures from one another, but it will be interesting to see how far and how fast they can move, because they have a sense of themselves that I think took most of us another ten or fifteen years to get a hint of. They have some idea of who they are and what's possible for them. The decisions they make are more carefully considered, wider-perspective decisions than I was able to make at those points, and it looks very good.

So, has anyone got questions on their mind about anything in this area? I'm willing to try to talk about what I've seen work and not work and what we've tried . . .

SHYNESS

Question:

I have an eleven-year-old son who is quite shy— not with family, with outsiders—and I had the same difficulty as a child. I want to help him out, but he's so shy I don't know what to do.

Tim:

You still have it, right? That's why it's hard to think about, but it also gives you an advantage in some ways. What you have to do is decide that you have to sacrifice yourself and that distress to help him out of his. You haven't had enough motivation to get out of your shyness yet, and this may provide it. What you have to do is work on it with him. It would be nice if you didn't have it, if it was out of the way, and you could be a nice clear counselor. What you have to do is go be shy together. That's one of the best things. And you have to fall apart with him.

NOT *JUST* A COUNSELOR

It comes back to one of the things I forgot to say. It isn't enough to simply be a counselor for our children. Many parents who are struggling being parents want to change the relationship into a counseling relationship, and it isn't. It's a tool you use in that relationship, but it isn't the only thing you do. You don't fall back on it all the time and abandon the other relationship, but it's a very useful thing.

You can use it here in this relationship. If you know the sorts of situations where embarrassment comes up for him, and probably for you too, you just have to go out there and be embarrassed together. You have to talk about doing things that would embarrass you both, and you have to tell him all the embarrassing things that have happened to you, places where you've been embarrassed similarly to the places you see him struggling with. In fact, it's a standard procedure you should do with your clients no matter what age they are—start working on it by letting them work by reflection; it's too hot for them to work on directly on themselves, but they can laugh about somebody else working on it, and you are perfect! He trusts you and you care about him; you've got the stability, you've got the caring in the relationship and you also have exactly the right thing to work on. So you have to find a way to let yourself feel all of that embarrassment with him around and enjoy it, and not get lost about it, not be ashamed of it. It's just embarrassment and it can be a lot of fun. You have to go do what will probably feel like stupid things, with him.

Most of us who have embarrassment, and we all have a good chunk of it, find ways to act to pretend we don't have it, to be smooth, to be relaxed and just a certain way, or in charge or proper. You have to give up those things, you have to give up the pretense of having any dignity. People that are embarrassed try to cover it by acting dignified in some way, and that's not really dignity at all. That has nothing to do with the dignity you have as a person. It's just a shield so you don't have to feel the embarrassment. You have to go out and play with that; if he can see you start to do it, he'll laugh as you do it, but it will be off his distresses. Eventually he'll be able to figure out things to do together and really enjoy it. Embarrassment, if it's not too heavy, and if there's someone there who isn't sunk in it, is fun to work on. You can get so that once you start laughing you can't stop. You'll be falling down in the bus writhing on the floor in laughter; I think it will shift. He needs someone to take the lead would be my suspicion, and it's something you can do. You'll get some benefit out of it too, I think.

TATTLING

Question:

I teach at school. About fifteen children come visit with me for an hour each session. One four-year-old this past month wants to get my attention by tattling—so-and-so did this, so-and-so did that. My first reaction was to have him re-direct himself to the children rather than come to me. That didn't seem to be working, so I tried to think about it some more. I thought maybe I could help him think positive things rather than negative things. I've been trying to work with him on that. I'm still not very satisfied with what I'm doing. Do you have any suggestions?

Tim:

I've some hunches. I wouldn't know exactly unless I was there with the child, and even there it takes a little while to figure out. My first hunch is that tattling is just a pretext, that the little one is trying to find some way to get someone to pay attention to him; everything else is irrelevant and any solution you propose is irrelevant. What's being sought after is your attention, and you have to find a way to give it; that is very hard in a group of fifteen. In general, you can't.

I don't know your situation, but in anything resembling public school situations I taught in, there's no way to do that. I've known people to find solutions. Among the best have been simply arranging to have half an hour after school with a different child every day, so that you have a chance to have individual attention on them; they have a chance to set up a relationship with you personally so it isn't just you and the class, it's you and individuals that know you. There you have a chance to find things out, to show them you care about them, to be interested in what they think, to listen to them. It's not a perfect solution.

There are ways to play with groups, but that person sounds like he's hunting for something in particular, there's something burning in there that needs attention and he's just attempting to find it. I would try to find a way to spend a little time with that one if I could. You may not be able to. That's one of the frustrations about working in public schools, or most schools, whether public or private. You see so much that could be done and yet you don't have the resources. You really don't, and you have to face the fact that you don't and figure out how to use the resources you have and how to gather more. Unless you face that early you will just feel bad all the time; you see these things and you can't touch them.

That would be my hunch about it. The other thing, if you don't have time to do that, is to play with it a little bit. You could tattle back. You don't want to take it too seriously as if there were content in it. I would doubt that there is. It's a pretext for something. Even just in passing you can pay attention to them by trading secrets or tattling on other people, so that they can laugh about this funny little thing they're stuck in.

TOUCHING

Question:

Earlier you were talking about touch and how important that is. I work in an after-school program and a lot of the young people want to wrestle and push. I can't seem to find a fine line between pushing that's OK and pushing that hurts somebody. One question is, how do you reconcile that need to touch with a child's right to their own body and to not be touched if they don't want to be touched, whether by an adult or by other children?

Tim:

I think the real question is not whether a child has that right and how much you're drawing the line between their private right and some public right to be close to them. It's more just recognizing that humans do like that closeness, are starved for it in general, are hurt by not having it. One of the ways they get hurt by not having it is by being so scared and so lonely and so hurt that they shy away from it. This is one of the most confusing things for anyone around children, who is trying to be thoughtful and not manipulate them: how do you recognize where they're stuck, where what they're demanding is coming out of their distresses, or where it's something they really want because it's their best thinking? This is where permissive child-raising misleads people, because it says you don't have to decide, that whatever they want is just fine. That's understandable, but it's inadequate; it leaves the child trapped in that distress by themselves. Touch is the one that's real scary in society at the moment, so I can understand why it comes to mind quickly, but it isn't all that different from a lot of other things that children make decisions on and adults get perplexed about.

When you see a child adamant on something, you have to think about it and you have to watch for the repetitive rigid re-playing of that particular pattern of behavior. If it's there, a little flag has to go on in your mind that they're stuck, that it isn't really their best thinking; well, it's maybe as far as their thoughts have gone, and it's their best thinking at this point, but they're not able to think about it well because of some rigidity there. Once you recognize that, that doesn't mean you storm in on them any more than you storm in on any other client. It does mean that if you're the one that recognizes it you're the one that can figure out some action to change the situation.

The child who avoids closeness has to have a chance to do something other than just run away every time. For an adult to move in, you have to be very careful because of all the things I've talked about that we need to work on. But you still don't have to be passive about it. The safest ways are a little hard for adults to get a handle on initially; you have to take over the "bottom" role of the relationship. You have to let them be the powerful one and you have to beg to be close to them. You have to wheedle and whine and beg and apologize, that you shouldn't need to, but I do need to, can't I please, I'm sorry I'll try to get over it but, but for now . . .

That role won't restimulate them at all. They'll love it. They'll look down on you and sneer and dismiss you and cast you off, and you crawl after them begging and pleading. They will laugh and laugh and laugh in the upper role, having the upper hand and not being forced to work on it in some way because somebody else says it's a good idea, but being offered an opportunity that they can take advantage of that's within their reach to get started.

They won't be fooled. This is another place people sometimes get a little confused in counseling. They're not going to be fooled by what you do in that role. They will recognize that role immediately. They won't confuse it with you or things you have to do together or things that need to be done. They will recognize you're playing a role and they will use it for a long time if you can play it well, and you'll find little variations on it.

I was using a variation this morning for someone who didn't want to be held; I simply gave her to someone else and demanded her back and we, the two of us, two adults, demanded to hold her— she's mine, she's my baby, she's important to me, you can't have her, and made the game that way. She could laugh and laugh and laugh about two people demanding her and wanting her and passing her back and forth.

You can find ways to do it. Almost always as an adult counselor for a young one, especially if you don't know them well yet, you try to go in underneath in that role where they still have the upper hand, and you're just trying to find a way to make the resources available enough that they can look at it.

You can't wait for reassurance as an adult counselor of a young one. You have to go ahead, not sit there and look hopefully and hope they'll smile at you and say, "Yes, that's good technique." They're not going to do that. They expect you to take the role. They expect you to keep that role and to play it as far as you can and not turn helpless in it. The more you can do that the more they can use you. That reassurance doesn't come.

(There's a lesson in there I think for us as counselors for adults also. We tend to keep looking for reassurance all the time from other adults. That's interesting, but I don't think it's necessary and it probably slows us down a little.)

All the work I've ever done backs up that people like closeness. They like that chance to be close to somebody who can think. (There *are* people who they shouldn't want to be close to, and they're right about that. It isn't, "Brian, this is another human body with a somewhat functional brain in it, and you should be close to it.") There needs to be someone there who can think about being close, who can think about them. Some of their objections to people are very well-founded and need to be respected, and you have to be thinking about that, too. But if there's somebody there who is trying to think about them and trying to think about being close and making the offer, anybody would leap at it unless a distress was in the way.

If a distress is in the way and I can spot it, then I can find a way to help start to loosen it. Then you can just turn around and watch what's happening and start experimenting. You don't have to worry about it working the first time, you can go ahead and loosen it up and have them walk away. OK, they walked away. They've done that every day for years now from people who have tried to make an approach. That's not horrible. He'll learn something from it and you can go on and try something else. But I would always come in from the underside like that, where they have a chance to step on you when you make a mistake rather than being stepped on by you when you make a mistake.

REJECTION

Question:

I work with thirteen children aged three, four and five. The thing that most perplexes me in working with them is why, at such an early age, they get so heavily involved in such complex social interractions. An example is that almost every day I'll hear someone say to me, maybe even more than one young person and more than one time, "No one wants to be my friend." They're trying very hard to be friends and it's very, very important for them, and they're asking me for help. I was rejected when I was a kid.

Tim:

It's amazing how early distresses get in there on our young ones. You can understand why psychology gets confused and hunts for genetic causes to things because it seems to duplicate itself generation after generation, almost from birth. I don't think it's that complex. The way they get the distresses, of course, is that they live with us. We may not be acting that way at them but we're showing that on our face and in the way we interact as adults. You mustn't think a child doesn't notice. Children notice very, very early and make some sort of sense of the oddness of us and our patterns. They're trying to figure out what's happening right from the beginning. They don't have to be a target of a distress necessarily; they just have to be witness to it, for it to come in as a distress and be recorded there. The harshness of it isn't the same as if they're a target, but it's still in there unevaluated. It doesn't make sense and yet it's frozen there.

It seems to me that every child arrives expecting there to be someone in shape to listen to them. They come out. They look around expecting someone to be what we think of as counselor. I haven't seen many children who have had much of that, and that has a very real effect initially. I've seen that separation and isolation on all of us and I see it on very small ones; they turn and look at us and too often we're not there. Our face may be there and maybe even our eyes are looking, but we're not quite there, and I think that's noticed.

I've noticed in very small ones, down to less than a month old, that they will not necessarily look at you as they work on something. They can't, they won't turn in your direction. You will try to be there, try to give them attention, try to help them notice that you're there and that there's some resource available, and they won't be able to bear to look at you.

I see this, of course, with all the adults I've ever seen co-counsel, that they don't look at their co-counselor. They stare off anywhere else, and also, at that moment when they look at their co-counselor, their counselor isn't looking at them. The co-counselor may have been looking at them ninety-nine percent of the time, but something goes by the window at the wrong moment and the client looks up at that moment and the counselor isn't looking. You can almost see a little hand grab at the heart of the client. The session changes. Some hope gets covered over by the restimulation. I think this not feeling someone likes them probably is growing off that soft spot from their early days.

I've worked with children from very early, and it's a big struggle just to try to get in close enough that they will look at me. I'm pretty good at working with children. I've done a lot of it with babies; I'm talking about one month old. I can stay there and I can be confident and I can be proud of their existence, which I am, and I can sound that way and look that way. They will struggle, and struggle, and struggle, and I'll ask them to look at me. It will be very, very hard for them to do; eventually they will look over sideways and take a quick glimpse and then be able to cry all the harder. But it is a very big struggle. I think that's a background, that's there, so that when they say nobody likes me they're asking a more general question.

Any time you're counseling with anyone, when they give you a specific hurt, they're telling you the fact of it that's on top that they're feeling at the moment. The hurt is probably larger. There's a more general context to it that you can go after for a stronger contradiction. You don't have to just look at the little piece they showed you. That's what they could get out to you from the middle of that distress. You can think wider and provide a larger contradiction than that. You can always offer yourself; if they come up and say "nobody likes me," you can say, "Oh, that's not true, I love you, I'm just so happy you're here with me. I like coming here every day and knowing that you're going to be here and that I get to be with you. I know they get grumpy over there—you get grumpy sometimes too—but that's all it is. It isn't that they don't like you, it's that something happened that got them grumpy and they will get over it and they'll be able to show that they like you again. But in the meantime, I never forget that I like you. You don't ever have to worry about that, and if it seems like nobody likes you, you come mention it to me and I'll remind you."

Part of what we need to do with our young ones is to provide them a way to understand what happens in the world, including the distresses that get acted out around them. We need to try to provide a picture, some way to make sense of the world as they gather enough information to form their own picture. One of the best tools I know of is the way Co-Counseling looks at the world, the way Re-evaluation Counseling is able to make sense of and make some cohesive model of all the things that happen in the world, especially about people—being able to talk to a young one about what goes wrong when somebody gets upset— that it's just an upset, it's no more serious than that; it's not going to last forever, especially our own.

Our children need to hear us apologize when we get lost. They need to know we know we got lost, first of all; they need to have some perspective that the world doesn't just go flip like that for no reason. That we know we got lost, that we're sorry about it and that we're trying to do things to make sure that happens less and less, and there will be a time when that will never happen again, that we will never act that way again and that we're going to work hard at that because it's important to us.

Explaining that model in terms of ourselves as well as explaining why our cousins do this or our grandparents do that, helps the young one make sense of and make decisions about how to handle the world.

The holidays are coming, and for a lot of us it means going home and gathering in the big family. And the big family has all the family distresses that we've started fighting our way out of. You need to warn your children about them if they're not terribly familiar. You don't tell them not to do things, you just tell them what it's like, that if you do this Uncle George will turn red and yell very loud. It's OK with me if you do it, but that's what's going to happen. You try to give them enough of the picture that they can make decisions. You try to fill in the best model you have of reality so they can use it while they construct their own.

In all of these snags and difficulties, another thing is that we have a tendency to abandon our children in a lot of ways, especially in places we feel badly. One of these is about relationships. We sort of want to push them out and let them go form their relationships. I think that's a mistake. It's always useful to have more resource when you're trying to form relationships. You can play a role in that for your children or other children. You don't just put them out in the yard together and hope they make it. They are both carrying distresses and they will get snagged in certain places. If there is someone around who understands that and can play a role in it so they don't just act it at each other, whatever you can do as a counselor there, the relationships form better. Our experience has been that the adults, no matter how badly they feel about themselves in this area, can play a useful role in helping the young ones—in arranging times for the~

to be together with this other person and their being nearby so they can help; to think about where the snags are and how to get around them; to get your young ones talking about where they get in collision courses with other young ones. All of those things make the relationship easier for the young one to figure out, and we can play those roles.

We carry this funny duality in that we feel like we have to interfere in all these places as adults, because that's what was done to us, and on the other hand we feel like we ought to stay out of the way because we can't really do anything useful; that this new clean child will probably do better by themselves than with us helping. That's just not true.

SIBLING CONFLICTS

Question:

Would you talk a little bit more about how to deal with the kinds of conflict and violence that come up between siblings?

Tim:

It's endless until you do something. Every distress is endless until something happens. That's the nice thing about distresses; they keep going on over and over in the same way, and parents pray that it won't happen today. You know, please don't let them do that today, not at Grandma's house, wherever. And of course it is going to happen, until something gets done. As I said before, if you can spot it and if you can think well enough to see the rigidity of it and the distresses involved, then you're the ideal candidate to figure out a way to loosen it up and change it, because the two people in there are too locked to be able to think about it in general, or at least you can't wait for them to figure it out. There's no reason to wait once you're aware of it.

What are their ages? (Six and nine.)

There are lots of things to do, but you have to go back and remember what's happening. You've got to go back and build this model of it because it's so restimulating. It's hard to keep track when it's happening unless you have something to refer to. In general what's happening is you have two clients. It seems like we tend to do this in relationships that we have for long periods of time, especially people we live with. We tend to try to get their help on our distresses by acting it out at them. So the young ones will act it out at each other, but neither one will have the resource to turn counselor for the other one usually. Occasionally it happens, but usually not, and so somebody has to get in there as counselor. Most parents long for a way to keep it from being acted out. That's really not the goal. It will keep happening as long as they have those distresses. What you really want, aside from not being restimulated yourself by it, is you want them free from those distresses.

Those things are really opportunities. Instead of praying it won't happen,.what you have to do is plan on it happening. You know it's going to happen, you know it always happens, so you ought to be able to plan an attack. If this happens, if I have these two clients with these distresses that get tangled in this way, and I know it's going to occur, what am I going to do this time? It means you getting in there (or somebody, you or the one that's there, so I imagine it will be you), and you have to go in as counselor in some way that they can make use of you. There are variations depending on how tight and how vicious the distresses are and how scared you are, and so on.

A good one to start with is when they're fighting over some object, which is a common one—this is mine, no mine, no mine, you had it last, it's my turn. You go in and grab it and run with it. What happens almost always is these two people that were ready to kill each other for this object, become fast allies immediately and come after you. You allow yourself to be trapped in a corner making stupid turns, so that they always corner you and tackle you and you hang on to it for dear life as they try to grab it from you, and you shriek annd moan and cry that it's your turn. They've had it for weeks and you haven't got a chance to play with it. Again, it's taking that role.where they get to show you how frustrated they are, how much they want it, without having to act it at each other; you're there, and because you don't have to react back at them, you can play with it and they can laugh and laugh and laugh.

That's one of the places you can play with a large group sometimes. There have been times when I have had a pack of fifteen just howling after me, and for an hour—it's good exercise as well—for an hour just running and letting them catch me and knock me down and struggling up and getting away, just barely. You run so that you're no more than six feet away from the pack. They will use that opportunity to safely show you how desperately they want it, if you can handle it and not be upset at them for it.

There's a strange thing that happens to all of us when we get lost in a distress and act it out, and that is we get blamed for it. Children feel this very, very heavily. They didn't mean to act that way, and yet they're blamed for acting that way. It's as if, here they were sitting nicely, playing sweetly, and some monster came up and took over their body and made them do this, and then the monster goes away and they're left there to take the rap. It wasn't their intention and they're sorry about it and they wouldn't do it again, but they're blamed for it. We all get blamed for having distresses that, in effect, we didn't choose ever to have. We'd love not to have them; we don't get much help in getting out of them, and we're blamed for having them. It makes it hard for a young one to show themselves to us, once they get blamed for the distresses they're carrying. How are they ever going to talk to us about them when we've yelled at them about them? It's one extra turn that just tightens it up a little more.

So I would go in and not be upset by the fact that they're upset with each other. If it's real hard, sometimes you hold them this far apart until they can't quite reach (I don't know how big they are, physically, compared to you), and let them storm. A lesson in this is that you try to get this work done as early as you can in their lives, you know, before you get frail by comparison. We've known lots of people who have taken these ideas and done a very nice counseling job with a pair of children, sometimes holding one in each arm and letting each one tell what it was like.

I've heard people arrange little things where the person can show how mad they are without damaging anyone—say getting sixty sheets of paper and balling them up and having two lines across the floor so they're five feet apart and just pelting each other and calling names. You can find different ways to play with it that removes the main restimulation so they don't sink each other at it. I've cheered young ones calling their folks names and calling each other names and say, "Oh, that was a great name, you really got them on that one, what are you going to say back?" and just letting them go ahead with someone not upset about it. That's the crucial thing, that there's a counselor in there who has perspective, who can keep that tone from freezing where they feel bad for being attacked and they feel bad for attacking but they can't stop. You get so you enjoy it actually. It really is fun once you stop taking it too seriously; it is an interesting challenge.

"DISRUPTIVENESS"

Question:

What do you do when children are disruptive? I've tried "time-outs."

Tim:

Well, I think that's a lot better than what was done last generation, but it doesn't address the problem. It is trying to cover up and suppress. The child doesn't disrupt because they mean to; they're trapped in the distress and showing it almost in desperation, usually, trying to get some help with it. They don't mean to be disruptive or harmful to anyone, and unless you can find a way to help them with that distress, everything else is a little bit cosmetic, trying to keep things going, to keep things going. Sometimes that's important, and once young ones have some idea that you will help them with their distresses and actually pay attention so they can talk and work on things and play with things, they're much more able to put aside the distresses that grab on to them, with the reassurance you will listen later. But initially, life is just desperate; they're hunting for a way. It's like every client who has never had a chance to discharge on most things and is willing to tell anybody in any situation, or to show it or act it out and hope somebody notices.

The "time-out" is gentler, as I said, than last generation's solutions, but it's still a punishment in some ways. It still carries that tone: If you're going to act that way you're going to go sit over there; it doesn't address the problem. I can understand its use, in desperation, when you don't know what else to do, but I think you can find better solutions.

One of the things that interrupts distresses for young ones especially well is physical closeness. You try to find a way to get there before they get so lost they have to act this out. You don't wait to see if they can handle it by themselves today. Once they start having trouble, if you watch them there are signs ten, fifteen minutes ahead of time, as they struggle with it and it starts coming out. You try to get there before then and just pick them up and cuddle them for a second. Just some contact will give them a bit of perspective, something to hang on to against the pull of that distress so they don't get lost in it so easily.

When I was teaching second grade, my working assumption was that the children arrived at school in the middle of a distress. It wasn't always true, but that was my working assumption, and it's fairly true. If it didn't happen at home, it happened on the school bus or in the school yard or walking in. I considered it my job to help them learn certain things. My job there wasn't counseling, I had a different goal there, but I would use everything I knew about counseling to accomplish that goal. I made the assumption that they were going to be lost when they came in and my first job was to get them out of those distresses enough they could learn.

I would do all sorts of things. Mainly, I would walk around, and it always turned out in the second grade classes that every single child would try to touch me as I came by. Almost all the girls and a few of the boys would grab my hand. The rest of the girls and most of the boys would hit my hand as I went by. That's as close as they could get to being affectionate. But they would all try for it. They would want to be close, and I would just go around and put a hand on shoulders, hand on heads, and it would make a very big difference to them. Even the most troubled ones, the ones who looked like they were having a real hard struggle in their families every day, could come out a little bit and look around. I would try to get there before the child got lost. I think you can figure it out unless you get too many children and then it is harder.

Physical contact works forever. I taught a calculus class when I was a graduate student, and all of the calculus sections took the same final in one big auditorium (if you went to a large university you know the sort of mass production that goes on). So we were scattered all over. During the final I would walk around and sit down next to my students and lean on them, sort of subtly, and put my arm around them and ask how they were doing. You could see them sort of surface and wake up from this intense desperation of working on this paper, and look around and then go back and work. It was a small test, but my students out-scored every other section.

INSECURITY

Question:

How do you counsel on the child's pattern of clinging to the mom? I have a four-year-old that clings.

Tim:

I think that is connected to the "not being sure we're out there" distress that I talked about. We all seem to have this distress. I mean, we steel ourselves and get over it and march on, but we all carry it. It's part of why we have trouble helping young ones work on it, part of why we can't pay attention to our young ones well enough to stop it from being passed on. What the young one needs to do is work on how scared she or he is, how scary it is for them for you to go away, whoever it happens to attach to; it isn't always mommy, but, given the way society is and the way things happen, it almost always is mommy.

They need a couple of things. They need some safety, which usually means you have to be there. And they need to look at the situation and not just huddle in and go numb (just bury their nose in your shoulder and not look out and not be able to discharge, but just hang on for dear life).

The most workable and the most common situation that occurs is that you have to go somewhere and somebody else is going to be with them. That's a perfect situation if that other person understands counseling enough and has worked on their childhood a little, so they don't get upset at the child for feeling this way, or they don't try to sympathize so much that they quiet the child pleasantly—it still stops the discharge.

If you have this situation, you try to allow half an hour to leave, and you just say, "I'm going to have to go soon. I'll be back." You need to provide all sorts of reassurance to them, because the fear isn't just that you're going, it's the fear that you will be gone, period. The sort of reassurance I try to give is that "Mommy will be back, mommy will always be back. She's never going to go away and not come back. You are one of the most important things in her life and she would do anything to get back here. If she gets lost and confused and doesn't get back when she's due back, we'll go find her." The fact that there's another ally who understands how important it is and who will help find mommy if mommy gets wandering around somewhere is also a useful contradiction, I think.

As parent, the contradiction is that you will always come back and that they will be safe in the meantime. You just need to say that you have to go soon. The other person needs to have probably just one hand between the little one's body and your body. That's all it takes to remind them of it, so they can't quite go numb and just cling there. They will shriek and cry and cry and cry for a long time; how long? No way to predict, but much longer than you would like, much longer than you would expect.

There's a general transition. The amount of time the young one needs to cry about it before enough comes off that they can see you go without being upset, gets shorter and shorter and shorter. You don't always have that much time to wait through it. Initially the length of time can be very long, so you have to go ahead and go. But whenever you can, you want to take advantage of the opportunity to work on that so that it gets easier and easier and easier for them. This comes up at all family workshops; every time parents go off to a session there's a chance to do that work.

PARTICIPATION

Question:

When we're in a group, if I'm not there my daughter participates fully, but when I'm there she just wants to sit on my lap and hang around me.

Tim:

It sounds closely related. What's necessary is for someone to want her to play and to not force her to, but to sit there and be persistently wanting her to, so that she gets to feel she would like to go play. She gets to feel that and yet gets to feel whatever the fear echoes in her mind about leaving you, and can work on it right there. It will just take some work. It will take some discharge, and then she'll be able to more easily go off.

We've seen children work through this a lot, usually lots faster than their parents do. What often happens is that the child is perfectly happy for mommy and daddy to go away, and mommy and daddy feel like the child doesn't care about them any more. They've been depending on this dependence on them for their reassurance, a little reactive reassurance. It isn't really what you want, but it's so much better than you felt like you had. There's somebody that deeply cares about you; stuck or not, they deeply care about you. So the parents have to work on the fact that this young one has a life of their own and will be independent and will be marching off. That's what you want. Then you get to work on your loss-of-loved-one feelings that are left over from your childhood, because I think that's where it grabs on.

HOLIDAYS, GIFTS, POSSESSIONS

Question:

(About Christmas holidays, Santa Claus, older siblings, sugar, gift-giving . . .)

Tim:

Well, where to start? Santa Claus . . . I don't think it makes sense to mislead our children, or anyone else, about any aspect of reality, and I don't think they need to believe it to enjoy it. If a custom is enjoyable, they don't have to be misled about it to enjoy it. I don't think it's necessary to mislead in those ways.

On gifts, on world possessions, on "mine"—that is a very large struggle that doesn't just have to do with children. It has to do with private property, it has to do with capitalism. It is not a small little issue. In general, nobody knows what makes sense after growing up in our societies. It is very difficult to figure out. Just the idea of "mine"—What is mine? What is ownership? In the family it has strange meanings—this toy belongs to the child but somebody else still decides when they play with it.

We are not good at talking about objects and ownership and use of. The basis isn't thought out or rational. Then add to it all of these other things—like gift-giving and the society pumping them to try to want everything possible. You have a lot of sessions to do with them wanting things. The fact that your young one doesn't want anything you'll give her is very nice, is perfect. It's a hint, it's as big a hint as she will ever give that you have to say "no," and that you have to work on the disappointment of you saying "no." Probably they will use that pretext to work on all the confusion around presents.

Presents are nice, not because of their mass or the cost or any of those things. I think presents can be very useful. They give you a chance to do something for someone that that person can't quite figure out how to do for themselves. That's the ideal gift. You think about them. What's something they would really like to do but can't quite figure out to do for themselves? It's really in some sense a direction. The good gift is popping them out of a place they're stuck and giving them new possibilities. That's one very good use for gifts. There are things people also just need; of course, that's nice, too.

There are ways to use gifts to help people grow and think and try out new things. The other mass consumption, the profit motive, marketing things, I think is lousy. Anyone who gets pulled into it has to have a chance to work on it. Children need a chance to talk about all these things, and so do you. You need to talk about Christmas. You need to talk about gifts—all of those things from your childhood, so that you can back off a little from it and think about it. You can figure out a way to put some real human contact into whatever holiday you're going to celebrate.

There's enough hint left over of thoughtfulness and caring in a lot of holidays, that you can find a way to use it and create your own tradition for your family that allows you to communicate. Maybe you sit down and tell stories about the coming of the children, their first years or how much you looked forward to them, or you trade stories of what you remember of your childhood. It can be a time when you sit down together.

Children love to hear stories of their parents' childhoods. Most parents can't think to do that, but your children want to know what childhood was like for you. They want to know you. We get so caught up in being ourselves presently that we ignore all sorts of facets of ourselves that they're interested in. In the holiday, everyone can sit down and get five minutes going around talking about something back in their childhood. You can do all sorts of things that will make the holiday useful and meaningful to them without having to follow along the beaten path. They will also need a chance to complain and discharge on things they have picked up in the society.

OVER-PROTECTEDNESS

Question:

Are you saying that there's no way for young people to get through childhood without getting sunk at Christmas, just because they live in the culture?

Tim:

Yes, there's no way to put them in some little, sterile insulated bubble somewhere. I don't think there's any way. I don't think that's our job anyway. Our job as parents is not to protect them from every possible distress. Our job is to provide them with opportunities to go out and learn about the world, to provide the resource to recover from distresses, and to help them avoid the ones they can't handle yet. We can do some of the judgement on timing—no large butcher knives until they're at least four-years-old—some independent judgement. The good parent is not the parent that somehow keeps them pure and clean. Life is too uninteresting if you try to do that. It's too uninteresting for the child. The child needs to go out and see the world, including the distresses that are all around us. They need help in understanding them, they need help in discharging the ones that catch them.

They get to really learn about the world and understand what's happening. They get some sense of their own power to recover, to run into the harsh edges of it and recover from it, to go out and hold their ground in it. I think that's closer to what our job really is as parent.

DIFFICULT SPOTS

Question:

I teach in a high school. At the high school we work with young people who have experienced failure in other schools. We find that when they are tested for specific thinking skills, that we often come across someone who is at their age level or above what's considered the norm in a lot of different areas, but in one very small specific area they might be ten years behind. Do you have experience with that phenomena? How it might come to be in a person's life? The established attempt to explain it is usually with an organic explanation, something to the effect that it's simply that they're missing some chips.

Tim:

I don't have a lot of experience there. My hunch is that there is a particular place where they got really hurt and they've never had a chance to learn in that area. That one place has just snowballed on them. If it's a place that comes up in school, if it's a part of learning and it got messed up by distress early in their struggle in public institutions, they would never get a chance to recover from it. First of all, schools are not organized in a way where anybody ever gets enough individual attention to fight through most things.

Even though you have many, many very well-meaning and dedicated people who try very hard to make schools work, the structure of them, the restrictions, the lack of funding, everything else connected with them, make them virtually unworkable. It's amazing how well we have all survived! Once a distress gets put into place, I don't see how it ever gets corrected within the schools. Most of the help comes from outside. If particular people don't have outside resources, if the family can't think, if they get upset about things, I'm not surprised that you find these pockets of distress there. Once the pocket is there, if that pocket of distress is in the wrong place, then it messes up a lot of school itself.

Our schools teach us this tiny little bit of something and condition us to feel helpless and incapable of doing almost everything. All the studies show that though we may know how to read, few of us do read anymore. We don't read books. Maybe we read a newspaper now and then. That's part of the conditioning that's gone on for all of us. Working in a high school, I think you have a tremendously difficult job to do.

I wouldn't confuse the area where they are struggling with any particular distress. My experience has been that often it's only accidental that this area of learning is disrupted by the distress. The distress has only the most remote connection with it. Once someone finally notices them enough and encourages them enough, is warm and supportive enough that they can start functioning in this area, everything else loosens up. Sometimes I've never been able to figure out the connection between the difficulties they exhibit in school and what they work on somewhere else. So you don't want to take the official analysis of the difficulty too seriously, but it is an indication something is wrong and some resource is needed.

CONTENT, NOT NAME

Question:

My partner and I are raising a child and we are both women. I find that when I go to the Day Care Center to pick A— up, the children don't know what to do with me, and I've done a poor job because of my own internalized oppression. They keep asking me the same questions every time: "Who are you?" "What is a 'co-parent'?" They're really just curious. If there is any kind of affection between us, then there's shock on their faces. I'd like to find a right way of helping them feel more comfortable with two women.

Tim:

The word "co-parent" isn't going to have any meaning for them. Finding a word is not going to be the solution to it. What you have to do is show you are caring for the child and for your co-parent. That's what will make sense to the other children. Show how much you care about them, how much you enjoy them, how much you look forward to being with them, and find ways to interact with them. Once everybody sees that, that makes sense. That's what everybody is hunting for—that commitment within the relationship, not some outside analysis or some label, but the human content of it. If you can find that and not be worried or embarrassed about what anybody else thinks (which means a lot of sessions for you), and just go ahead and make that your goal, I don't think you'll have any trouble with the children at all. The adults have picked up more of the distresses of this society, and it's a different struggle. You have different tools. You can talk and you can help them work on it, but for the children it's showing them the content to the relationship that will make the difference, I think.

IMMEDIATE COPING AND LONG-RANGE GOAL

Question:

Given that schools are so awful and that we have compulsory education, what does a parent do when sending their child into the system? How important is it for us to work to abolish compulsory education?

Tim:

This is a big question because, of course, the school system is part of the society in which it exists. All of the irrational pieces of the society get played out in the school system. You can't change the school system or the idea of education the way you want to without changing the whole society. It's one piece. You can't pull on it without the rest of it clinging to it.

The job really is re-making all of the ways we interact, the whole society itself. Only when we get a chance to do that well can education really become what it could become and what we know it could be—a mechanism to help people discover the universe, to figure out how to interact with each other, to figure out the way the physical environment works, to learn all of those things as a set of channels that they get to choose from to find the information they're interested in at the moment; not being compelled to learn certain things and being compelled to memorize rules and to follow the instructions of certain people unthinkingly, and all of those things that you know are part of current educational process.

I think we can have an effect on the educational system now. I don't think we have to wait until then. You can play a role in it. You are discouraged from doing that. Parents are discouraged from doing anything except dropping their children off at the school and picking them up responsibly at the right time. Other than that they're not supposed to be very interested or play a role. But most schools are full of people who are starved for additional resource, who work in the schools because they're trying to make them work, who want them to be good things even though they get lost in their distresses. You can find allies within any school. You can volunteer and provide resource.

One of the things that makes schools so harsh and makes even the best-motivated, intelligent, well-meaning people get lost, is they are just starved all the time for resource. They are given thirty children and very little resource to do the things they want to do. If you get in there and volunteer just for a couple of hours a week, you can start making a difference, partly because you can listen to the teacher talk about her discouragements and her unhappinesses and you can support her ideas. You can give her your model of the world as something to think about when she gets discouraged.

It's still going to be a tough battle. Re-making the educational system is re-making all of society, but we can make differences where we can get our hands in. The more we do that the easier the big changes will be when they come; more people will be understanding already.

THE PALO ALTO SCHOOL

The other thing is saving our young ones in the meantime. We started our school for the young ones that I mentioned earlier, and we did this because the parents could not find good schools. The first longing was that we could find a school that was as good as we knew it could be, and people hunted all over for a long time before they gave up on that one. The second hope was that we could find someone who could do this for us, who would be smart enough, know enough and could do this job that we knew could be done better than we could do it. And people hunted a long time before they gave up on that one. We finally faced the fact that we were the people who knew what was possible, and so we were the people who were going to have to make it happen.

We did that, and we had six to ten children for a few years for three or four days a week, three or four hours a day. We tried different things. Our initial idea was simply to have a place where the children would be free to show themselves and the adults would not interfere with discharge. That was it. Those were the enunciated guiding principles initially. There were other ideas in the backs of some of our heads, but this was what we could agree on; it was clear enough.

What happened was, once we got there and once the children got some idea things were safe, the children went to work. They would just take advantage of the resource and have session after session after session. Any time the staff had had good sessions the week before, the children went ahead and worked on new things. They would smell the additional resource. We often worried about it; we didn't want to be manipulating the children into something. We'd keep trying to look at ourselves to make sure we weren't doing that.

We tried different rules at different times to make it possible for the staff to function. We had to interrupt certain behavior. One rule was that you didn't crash trikes. A little one came up once to one of the staff members, came up beside her and talked about this rule and was reminded, "Yes, that was a rule." Then the little one rode down forty feet away, turned around and rode straight into the staff room, and crashed the trike. He was just trying to get enough attention to go ahead and work on something, trying to wave this big flag in the face of somebody. So we were eventually reassured that it was not just our idea, that the young ones were able to make use of it and go forward.

The children that we had for a length of time worked on all sorts of things. First of all, they worked a lot on how they felt about themselves. That seemed to be one of the earliest things—troubles with the way they were feeling, failure around themselves, what they couldn't do, powerlessness, those things. They worked on their relationships with others, their family, the staff and the other children. They worked on the places they had difficulty in learning out in the environment, interacting, learning to read. There was a general progression. There were lots and lots of sessions. They started functioning differently.

INTO THE PUBLIC SCHOOLS

Eventually it seemed to us that there were two logical choices: one, to continue expanding the school and take more and more people, so that it didn't stay some weird little experiment, some elitist enterprise. We didn't have the resources to do that. The other thing was to go in and take over the school system. We sent a lot of people into the school system, but it happened mainly after these children left our little experiment and went out to the public schools.

People were worried that we were growing little hothouse plants. These children were going to be frail and spindly and unable to handle the outside world. So when children wanted to go to summer school, the public summer school, we figured it was a good experiment. That summer school was not as harsh as the other schools; most of the time you had some choice about things. So they went off. And they liked it.

At that time they were talking about the public schools as "the place where you had to do what they told you." That was their phrase for it. They went and liked it because it had all sorts of resources. It had microscopes; it had all of the things that they never saw around the little hovel where we operated.

(If anyone ever wants to run a school like ours, they're wonderful and they're impossible. There are real difficulties. There are financial difficulties—you over-charge the parents, you starve your staff, and you lose money. There's no way around it. There are difficulties in your relationships with the adults involved in the school—you run into "blue-page" problems all the time. My main part of the enterprise for many years was helping to clean things up. The basis of the relationship was a co-counseling relationship, and yet people would start getting pulled into expecting other things—"You have my child and you haven't helped them work on that." Expectations would come up, money problems, very complex things.)

It was a struggle all the time, and it finally ran out. We ran out of children actually, and we were also running out of steam. It was kind of convenient.

HOW THEY HANDLED THINGS

I guess all of these children are now in public schools. Not all of them went immediately to public schools; one or two went to alternative schools. They are all doing excellently. They don't seem to consciously think about how they do it, but they are well-liked, they are successful, they are looked up to and looked to for their thoughts about things. Judgement is checked with them in interesting ways. Harshness is not acted out at them very much by other young people. They can interrupt harshness in other young ones very deftly in very nice ways.

Closer to your question, it seems as though they are never target of harshness from the system. They will have lousy teachers; they'll sit in class and the teacher will go kerpow, kerpow, kerpow; hit every child seated around them and never aim at them. They have acquired, whether they consciously understand it or not, something that allows them to exist there and avoid most of the harshness of it and gain from it. They are able to handle things.

That was my hunch initially, that if we could get them through a few years and help them get distresses off and get them the tools to handle themselves a little, they could handle nearly anything. It looks like that's true. It did take us a lot of work, a lot of struggle, a lot of sessions for ourselves and them, but it looks like you don't have to go into the public schools as victim. You can go in at six or seven and have enough going for you, enough perspective on yourself, that you can manage even the irrationalities of that system fairly well. You can be making gains as you go through it, as opposed to how most of us had to struggle and try to hold even at best.

So I think there are things we can do in the meantime for our young people as well as for the schools. When you go in and do something for the schools, it isn't just for your young ones; you make a difference for the whole class. It's very good to make that effort and see the effect that we have, to see our ability to do that. Ultimately, yes, we have to throw the whole system out, it's true.

CONFUSIONS IN COUNSELING

Question:

Would you talk about the place in counseling young people where it looks like a lot of people get confused. I'm talking about paying attention to them, thinking about them and counseling them on an area as opposed to begging them in every way you can think of to make them cry. It looks like people get confused there.

Tim:

We do get confused in counseling children. Part of what happens to a lot of us is that we get desperate about it. We understand a child is hurt, and we urgently feel that we have to help them get through this. It is the adult's urgency about the distress. This shows itself in family workshops. Parents always want their children to work on this thing. Children never choose that to work on. That isn't what's important to them, that isn't what's messing up their life, but it's what's messing up the adult's life. The adult is worrying, feeling guilty about it, and of course the adult needs to go work on that.

We have a number of confusions like that that lead us to do strange things as counselors, that lead us to push, to have them work in certain ways that don't work well, that really undermine the safety of the session and remove our conscious thought and support for the person who is trying to work.

Some adults get fascinated simply by having a child discharge. It's such reassurance to them to think something is moving that they will try for the discharge without thinking about the client. Of course the client is the important person. The discharge is a sign that the process is working and important in that manner, but it's only important in the context of your being a supportive ally to that person. If you're in there trying to restimulate them, which it almost gets down to, trying to keep them on the edge so they're still feeling bad enough to cry, you're making a mistake. You're losing the relationship you're trying to build with them. If a child is working on something, you don't go do the thing they don't like over and over and over again so they can cry, any more than you would do that with a co-counselor, (though I've seen that with adult co-counselors, too).

The one I remember is someone in a group who was fairly new to counseling, getting up to take his turn and working on loneliness and feeling separate by trying to get the group to act badly at him. Then he tried to show that he could take it, that he was tough enough, instead of using the group for warmth and support to contradict the way he felt. He was going to try to do battle with it, setting the group in opposition. Such things miss where we're trying to go. They are believing that distress in some way is the important thing rather than trying to find the contradiction to it, trying to find the way for the client to feel stronger and more positive and more powerful in doing battle with it. For an adult with a young one, you're not trying to go in there and rub their face in it. You're trying to give them the support and the warmth so that they can do battle with it.

People probably get confused watching me and a few others. We will go in to a child who has sort of collapsed in on themselves, I mean, gone numb on a shoulder of a mother or a father. I will go in and put a hand between the two. What we're trying to do is remind them of the safety of the situation with a parent there and yet let them keep aware of the distress that they've gotten lost in. We're trying to pull them back where they can look at the distress instead of just suffer in the middle of it. I think that may be where people get confused; they don't quite understand what we're trying to do.

I have trouble saying these things clear enough all the time, so I try to say them in different ways. You'll notice I've repeated myself about twelve times on four different topics already tonight. I keep trying to say them in different ways in answers to different questions just to see if I can't say it well enough eventually that it will be held in minds as you go out and try to work with young ones. It helps for me to keep trying to find ways to say it freshly. It helps me to think about it as well as helps the communication. This is one of the places that we struggle with. It's just because we have so much work to do ourselves in order to think easily about children. We keep getting confused in it.

There are very well-meaning efforts. I often feel badly going in and interrupting them and changing them, and I try to find a way to do it without invalidating the adult who's trying. They are trying something that's hard for them. They're making a big mistake, but they're trying something, and you have to find a way that they can keep trying these things. You will make mistakes; we all do make mistakes. We continue to make mistakes. That's fine. You just mustn't get stuck trying to justify them or prove that a mistake was not a mistake. You have to look at them and go on and figure out new things.

PHYSICAL FORCEFULNESS AND VIOLENCE

Question:

I have a four- almost five-year-old and I have a question about what I perceive as his trying to gain some power. He is into bumping and pushing a lot with his tricycle. He won't do it to me, but he does it to almost everybody else. I see it as a way of experimenting with power, of getting attention and of learning how to act in the group situation which is fairly new to him. I'm feeling uncreative about ways to help build his power and differentiate his power from violence, because he's enamored with strength and power. How do I direct that and give him his power?

Tim:

It's a little hard to tell from this distance, but I know some things around those issues that might be useful to you. One of the questions connected with this is just the idea of physical force. Children love being physically forceful. We lose that as we get older. We get talked out of it, we get scared out of it, we get shamed out of it. Women get it taken away from them much earlier than men, but very few of us ever get a chance to find out how to really use our bodies and how to keep them useful to us throughout our lives. So it's this funny struggle to try to get in shape, figure out what weight we should be, and all of these things we stay confused about. I think we get scared about physical force, partly because of this and partly because physical force, violence, was aimed at us. There's a very useful piece of being able to be forceful, very forceful, and it's very distinct from being violent.

I have never seen a young one being violent except for distresses. I don't think there's a lack of understanding that it's always been a distress where they go wild and start slugging or scratching or biting, whatever the particular form is. That one isn't an issue of understanding.

He may be starved to rough-house with somebody, with you. If he's hesitant about doing it you may have to initiate it. You may have to get down and wrestle with him, and you may have to have a lot of sessions before you do that, so that you're at ease, so that you can be thinking through it and not get too scared in the middle of it. Long-range, you need to have enough sessions so that you can enjoy it, because it's a lot of fun. It's a lot of fun to be close without having to treat each other as fragile creatures, to really tussle around.

Pillow fights are wonderful. It is very useful to a young one to have that sort of contact and be able to exert themselves and not be careful all the time while they're doing it. It's a nice way to end the day, to have a place and a time to have a pillow fight and a tussle at bed-time. Young ones can relax so well after having that closeness and being able to exert themselves, so well that they can put aside the distresses of the day and relax and go to sleep.

If you start experimenting with him you'll find out a lot of things about it that will let you understand what's happening. It may have something to do with power. I wouldn't count on it. I think it may be closer to the idea of social interaction, his not knowing what to do, and so having to bump into things. I think what I talked about earlier about helping him form relationships is something you can do. If he hasn't had a lot of social contact you need to have a group. Have two, three or four children over, with you with them all the time. You lead the interaction initially, so they have a chance to meet each other and interact with each other with somebody who can play counselor, with someone who can keep their attention out well enough that all the distresses don't immediately bubble up and get acted out at each other. I think you'll learn enough to figure out the next steps to do.

PLAY DAYS

I should mention the Play Days that have been done in Seattle and elsewhere. We keep doing them in different places. Young people and their folks and some non-parents gather every so often for three or four hours of play, of little sessions, adults getting to run off for mini-sessions. People learn a great deal because there's that extra resource around. You're not there trying to figure it out by yourself, having to battle your past and the restimulations and all of those things alone.

Thank you for coming. I hope you all stay interested in using counseling with young ones. It is a very useful thing to do. It will have far-reaching effects on you and those young people, and it's one of the most enjoyable things you could ever do. Thanks.

QUESTIONS AND ANSWERS

An Open Question Session
Boston, Massachusetts, USA
April, 1982

COMPETITIVE SPORTS

Question:

Would you talk about competitive sports, both playing and being a sports fan? What do you think makes sense about it, and where do you see people caught in distress?

Tim:

There is a part of competition that is useful. I think most of it is not. Most of it is a reflection of the isolation we all get put into and that gets played upon by our economic system and by our society. You are supposed to make it independently. The idea that you are supposed to cooperate to accomplish something comes in a distant fourth or fifth among the ideas that are impressed upon you. It's told to you only when the teacher needs you to do something. You get a projection of the aberrations and the difficulties of the society we're imbedded in, and all of that is hurtful.

What is useful about competitive sports is the challenge for you to excel, for you to try to do better than you ever dared try to do before, to not sit back and play it safe and act scared. So far there's nothing else that can deliver you that challenge except another human being. Nothing else is smart enough to see where you are and try to make you stretch. The way competition works well is not when you're trying to beat somebody, but when you're trying to make them stretch farther than they could before; not when you get the shot clear out of their reach so they have no chance at it, but when you put it just out of their usual reach, so that if they try as hard as they are able to, they can do it. That ever-present challenge makes a lot of sense and people thrive and prosper.

But it's hard to do because we all got beaten. Every one of us had older children around who had gotten beaten and they were waiting for us to play so they could beat us, could pass on this hurtful legacy. So you have to go back and work on what it felt like to be beaten all the time. Part of learning to play with young ones is learning to let them win, to let them work on this early instead of waiting until they are in the position where we adults find ourselves. You get to face and contradict a lot of that wanting to win so bad yourself because you know you could, at last.

On being an observer of competitive sports, there is something nice about seeing people excel. The physical coordination and the teamwork can be very useful and beautiful on occasion. That's about two minutes out of every game. Part of what hooks us is wanting to see examples of that. You wait for those plays. They are almost worth the two hours you wasted. Not quite, and you worry about it every so often. There is a hunger to see people function that well and function together that well. There are also all sorts of fears that keep us from trying to do it ourselves. I think everyone has to look at themselves and see where she or he gets stuck. I don't think that you shouldn't ever watch competitive sports, because there is a usefulness to them. There are times when watching something like that can light up the day and the week and the months afterwards.

FEARS

Question:

I work with a twelve-year-old boy who is growing up in a family where feelings are not talked about or dealt with. He's learned to see adults in certain patterned ways. Where I've gotten stuck is feeling like there are a lot of things that aren't that important to me but are important to him, like not swearing. When I've been casual about them, I've felt that so much fear was brought up in him that at one point he could have potentially done something really dangerous. I'm wondering what one does with a situation like that.

Tim:

Any time you're in a situation with someone and you know there are certain restimulations that will drive them wild, in whatever way, you have to always remember what they are. Once you have that information about them, you shouldn't ever forget it or hope they won't be restimulated "this next time." Depending on the relationship, how much time you have, and the situation, you decide either to work around it to accomplish the things you need to accomplish without running into it, or you decide to deal with it, to find a way to lighten it up and let them discharge on it. In your situation, I would deal with it. Something like swearing is ideal. Let a swear word slip out, then be apologetic about it. Don't be casual about it. Play out a caricature of his fears about it. The more precisely you know his fears about it, like if he got hit for saying things like that (which is not uncommon), the more precisely you can play out a caricature of it to make it light. Look around as if he were going to hit you as soon as it slips out, or you can plead with him not to beat you for it. You'll be crowding him out of his role in the fear. You'll be able to find lots of ways. You're trying to make it different enough from the way he faces that stuff usually, but still be referring to it. You're playing with the balance of attention in yet a different way. You're trying to contradict the distress and yet not pull attention away from it, by still hanging on that one topic. Also you're trying to put him in the powerful role about it, you're the one pleading not to be beat. You're trying to get him out of the helpless victim side of it, so he can discharge it more easily.

OPPRESSIVE COMMENTS

Question:

Do you have any ideas on how to interrupt oppressive comments by young people, especially towards each other?

Tim:

In some ways it's not too different than with adults, in that there are a thousand different ways to do it and you have to figure out which ones have the best chance of accomplishing something. When you say you want to interrupt it, you must ask yourself why you want to interrupt it, what do you want to accomplish? If there's somebody there that's being hurt by it, you want to stick up for them and make sure it doesn't go on. You're trying to interrupt somebody being victimized by it where they can't quite do it themselves. That's one thing. If you want to help somebody think about what just came out of his mouth, because that doesn't come out of anybody's mouth unless they are lost in a distress, that means you want to help them work on it and get it discharged.

If that's what you want, then don't just slam them with it, because they won't think about it and they won't discharge on it that way. They'll get tight and defensive or tight and guilty, and nothing will move and they're just as likely, if not more likely, to do it again as soon as you're gone. You want to find a way that they can question it themselves, laugh about it. You want to contradict the tensions, to jiggle it somehow.

With young people, making oppressive comments is often not the same as adults doing it. It is very often not frozen so heavily, but is often an experimental mimicry of adults. There is an attempt to play with it. I don't know the exact situation you're talking about so I can't be sure, but often there is an attempt to play with it that doesn't have that dead, steely tone to it that you hear in adults. There is a little zing to it. They are trying to get somebody to put enough attention on it so they can laugh about it and not just be in the middle of it. It's hard and scary to hear that stuff go on around them. Young people hear it going on around them and it freezes in fear on them, even if they are not the target. Just to hear it is scary, to hear somebody else that unaware of somebody, to be that hateful, hostile, whatever that tone is, puts in a distress. So they are trying to bring it out in the open somehow, and very often, if it's that light, sort of zingy tone, you can play with it lightly too. If you don't get heavy-handed about it, it's much easier. Find a way to call it again. "Say what?" — and they may not be able to say it again, but you'll see a grin. You have to do it not looking upset.

Find some way to put attention to it without any heavy-handed disapproval. Nobody makes oppressive comments and doesn't know it's wrong and doesn't wish they had a way not to say it. You don't have to lecture them about it; that isn't the way out of it.

Sometimes, on rare occasion, you do have to step in and stop it. It's real heavy and harsh, the person isn't thinking about it, it already has that steely tone and somebody's being hurt and victimized by it. You interrupt and say, "You're not going to say that here. I don't care what you think, I don't care what you feel, you're not going to say that here." No buts. You don't put a threat behind it, it's just "You're not going to. It is not correct for anybody to be talked about with that tone of voice or in words anything like that. I wouldn't let anybody talk about you like that and I'm sure not going to let you talk about anyone like that." Lay it out straight. Not mad at them, not after them, but this is the way it is. You try to give as wide a perspective as you can, but you stop it. And sometimes that's not enough and you get physical. You do what's necessary.

PARENTS' SPECIAL SITUATION

Question:

Could you talk about the division between parents and non-parents, and why we have divided up separately for this part of the evening, and what's going on in their meeting?

Tim:

They're talking about us in there, saying, "Those people don't understand." Being a parent is a very special thing. The isolation of it is immense. It's very hard to understand that. Nobody knows what it is to be a parent until it's too late. That is strictly, literally true. No matter what children you borrow for how long, no matter how many people you know, no matter what you do to prepare yourself, it's different. And it's more. You need to understand that it's going to be more than you've ever expected and not be scared that you've miscalculated when you get there. It's part of the role. The nearest thing I can think of is what someone wrote about computer programming. One of the messes of the industry is you can never figure out how long it's going to take to program something. This person's rule of thumb is it will always take 60% more time than you figure on, even using this rule. It's the sort of problem you can't quite get a grasp on. I don't know why it's like that, but it really is like that.

Parents need the chance to meet together with other parents where everybody there knows what it's like and they don't have to be careful about it. We're all well-meaning, we want to know, but we don't. We haven't been there, we haven't fought those struggles yet. It's very helpful to have that safety. There are also some things to talk about with non-parents.

COMBATTING PARENTS' ISOLATION

Question:

Do you know of ways that both parents and non-parents have worked together to combat some of the isolation of being parents?

Tim:

I can't give you a recipe to make it work well, but I can give you some examples. One parent who is a single mother with one child was fighting through some distresses that made her upset easily. Anything the daughter did set her off, and her upset was always aimed at the daughter. Mother knew it wasn't right, but it was heavy enough that she didn't control it when it happened. So what she worked out with her counselors was that the daughter could call any of them any time at all, day or night. There was an agreement there, which momma hated but agreed to, that as soon as she got upset, she had to stop and wait for daughter to call somebody.

So daughter would start crying as the upset came, and would say, "Where are the phone numbers?" Mother, hating every moment of it, would hand over the phone numbers. They'd dial, and daughter would say, "Mommy's getting mad at me again," hand the phone over to mother, who by that point was thinking very differently. It took a lot of guts and commitment to do that, but it made a real difference.

Momma could cry and cry and cry about getting stuck in that position again, because it's not what she wanted, it's not what she ever intended, but she didn't yet have the resource not to get stuck there. She needed that counselor right then. There are things you can do like that.

We've found that trying to counsel your own children is very hard in isolation. You need somebody else around. As you try to counsel your children, it's nice to have your counselor there, so you're not doing it in isolation. Somebody else is listening, watching, appreciating your efforts, and is someone you can go have a session with afterwards.

One other thing that can be done (and this is one of the things we like to talk about with non-parents) is for you to form relationships with young people. It's a very unusual idea in our society. You as adults need relationships with young ones for your own health, for their health, for their parents' health. These are relationships with the young ones, not with their folks. It will benefit their folks greatly, but it's between you and the young one. The young ones need it because you don't have the same distresses as their parents. They get to try things their parents are afraid of. There are all sorts of opportunities that open up with you that aren't there when they're with their folks. Your distress isn't any better, it's just different, so they get to try things out a little differently.

If you can, think about being a permissive counselor for a young one. By that, I mean really paying attention to them and following *their* instructions at least until the instructions lead them into danger. Suspend your judgment on anything except that, and just be with them. Let them experiment with the world and try things out on a consistent basis. If you can do it once every two weeks so that they can count on you being there, it's very, very helpful to everybody involved. It will help you remember your childhood, it will help you counsel better, it will help you think better about being a parent. It will help the parents because there is somebody else that cares about their child and that will try to think about them.

The isolation of being a parent is tough. It's rough also to have it appear that you're the only one thinking about the child. That's very, very difficult. What happens if you make mistakes with this person that you care about? There's nobody else thinking about them. That's the picture a lot of parents carry all the time. If somebody else is making a consistent effort in that direction, it loosens things up a lot. The time that you will be with the child, they will be able to relax enough to do something else. They won't constantly be needing to check and see if things are okay.

So, if you can find a way to do this, do it. It doesn't have to be a child in counseling at all. It can be any child in the neighborhood. You will find that it's greatly appreciated by that child's family.

You will have another problem shortly after you start — that is, how to keep them from taking over your life. And that's all right. You will find out certain things you need to know. I once lived in a neighborhood where there were thirty-six children and we simply opened the house. I would have play-day every day with thirty-six children. I organized them and taught them how to play together and the older ones looked after the younger ones and we made it work. But it took up most of my time for a month. I treasure that. I learned a lot, it was well worth it. I've never regretted a bit of it. But it took a lot of effort.

STEP-PARENTING

Question:

Would you talk about being a step-parent?

Tim:

You shouldn't try to act like a parent. The relationship has to be separate, independent of a parent's role. You can't take over that role. It doesn't make sense at all.

More than that, it doesn't work. Lots of people try to make it work, but you can't come in as a replacement. You have to try to find a way to get in very good, open communication with the young ones in the family about who you are and what kind of relationship you want with them. It's got to be much more of a symmetrical relationship than being parents starts out being. Talk about your relationship with their parent. All of that has to be open and communicated back and forth a lot so that you can figure out the relationship. It's very useful to the children to have you come in as a step-parent. To have somebody else around as resource, especially someone who has different distresses than the ones they've grown up around, can be very helpful. But you mustn't confuse it with being a parent. It is a different sort of relationship.

PREPARING FOR PARENTING

Question:

I'd be interested in suggestions for working on thinking about becoming a parent.

Tim:

I would suggest you borrow a baby overnight. That will give you lots of things to think about. You also need to think about why you want to be a parent. Ask all those questions. What are you going to do when things go wrong? What are you going to do if you feel you have an ugly baby or if your baby doesn't seem to like you? Or what happens if your child's a bully? All of these horrible things that could happen. They won't, but all of those fears reside in us, and they should be faced ahead of time so when the young ones get there, you have nothing but unreserved admiration for them and love and happiness that they're there. All of the little distresses from your own infancy, all of the things that you've picked up beforehand shouldn't be there. It shouldn't be their job to contradict those distresses in you.

Unfortunately, a lot of us look especially to babies to contradict our discouragement. They've got to be happy for us, otherwise the day is miserable. It's nice that it works that way sometimes, but the onus shouldn't be on them to do that job. So you want to get all of that cleared out. You want to make it so that the young one comes and has a chance to be her or his own person from the very beginning, doesn't have to try to live up to anything that you want at all. You should be pleased that there is a new creature in the world and you're lucky enough to be around to watch, to form one of the first relationships they ever have, to watch what it means to be a developing human being, to enjoy the whole thing.

It is one of the two most interesting things in the world, to help a new young one develop. The other one is working with large groups of people on causes that move us all forward. Those are the two most interesting things I can think of. It takes a great deal of effort and energy.

COUNSEL THEM WHEN YOU ARE UPSET?

Question:

I have a question about parents counseling children, something about a power relationship. I know that when someone tries to counsel me when I'm acting distressed but they're also restimulated, it can be very oppressive. It seems to happen a lot with parents and other adults who are around young people. They're irritated and restimulated out of their minds. You know that the child needs to discharge so you try to counsel them, but the real message the child gets, I would think, is powerlessness and manipulativeness. So what does an adult do when they're not really in a position to counsel?

Tim:

Then you don't do it. You don't want to tell them, "Boy, am I mad now, so I'm not going to counsel you," and you don't want to pretend you're not restimulated out of your mind and try to counsel them, because you can't. There are a couple of things you can do. First of all, we always recommend you have sessions on your childhood and on children for six months before you try to do very much as a counselor for children. It doesn't work otherwise. But you still find yourselves in these positions, even after that six months of hard work, and sometimes you don't do anything. When two children are fighting and you're so upset all you can do is add your upset to the pot or smash them down so hard it suppresses their upsets, you let them fight. If it's their fighting that's restimulating you so badly, you go *watch* the fight and find out exactly what's restimulating for you. If it's two- and three-year-olds, they're not going to hurt each other. They fight every day. It's distressed, and it'd be nice if they didn't fight, and it'll be good when you help counsel them out of it so they don't, but it isn't a catastrophe today, even if it's gone on every day for a while.

Gather-In and Open Question Session
Seattle, Washington, USA
October , 1982

TV

Question:

How much should young people watch TV?

Tim:

I think the question is different than that. The question is, what are they watching? Most of television is not watchable. Most of television is not watchable by any of us. We get so shut down that we'll sit down and look at anything part of the time. A very large part of television is the playing out (sometimes skillfully) of someone's distresses as an art form or a commercial form. Very often, all of the stories, all of the plots in every weekly serial, are locked in distresses, and if it's done just right it hooks you so you have to go back next week to see it again. Some of them are very obviously locking distress in.

I have friends who are hooked on horror movies. They are too terrified to get in their car after a movie, but the next one that comes to town, they'll go back. Some of the junk on TV is almost that heavy, leading almost that directly into your terror and fears.

A lot of it is aimed at your distresses, more than you've probably been able to think about. It doesn't make sense simply to let a child watch it. It doesn't make sense simply to disallow it either, for you to step in as final arbitrator. There's a curiosity about it. They may be already hooked on it. Just breaking it off for them may not be the most effective thing to do. It may restimulate all the other times adults make decisions for them without consulting them and without thinking about them. The fact that you're trying to think about them may not make it different enough that they can tell.

You *can* sit down and watch something with your child, and not just go frozen-eyed too. You can all remember freezing in front of the television as a child, can't you? (You may still do it.) Mom or Dad came through the room, said something or asked you to do something. Five minutes later enough of your attention grabbed that sound — oh! — and you knew what they said five minutes ago, but you were so locked in that no thinking was going on separately.

When this happens, you are, in effect, not even thinking about what's going on on the television; you're in it. You're jumping along in that restimulation. (laughter) I've seen it work for parents (and others) to sit down with the young ones and not just watch, but talk about what's happening. Sometimes make fun of it, sometimes predict what will happen next. Make light of it, laugh about it so they can laugh about it, too, and not be frozen in it.

If you're in good shape, if you counsel on a lot of things as a parent, if you've worked on all sorts of things from your childhood so that you can actually be an aware counselor and not just be a stiff, authoritative adult, there is a point in saying, "You can't watch that." Don't expect them to go quiet and say "OK;" expect them to be upset, and stay there to help counsel them out of that upset. There are all sorts of things that will be restimulated, and they need a chance to work on it. Your deciding it isn't the end of the process. It's the start. It will give them a chance to work on all of the distresses that have been pent up there; some of them will be about adults making decisions for them, some of them will be about the frantic addiction for that particular TV program. You have to give the young ones a chance to work out these things, and not *just* make the decision for them. Let them talk about why they want to watch it, how important it is, what they think about as they watch it. You know if they recount the plot to you eight or ten times after they see it that there's something built up there, and you need to move in and give them a chance to discharge on it. I'd sit down and watch it with them first, because until you do, you won't really know exactly what's got hold of them. You need that information. You can't just decide about it. The more precise information you can get, the better.

GUNS

Question:

What about children and guns?

Tim:

There are many forms of the old question: should they have guns? It comes back to that somehow. Should they have oppressive things? Things that scare us? I guess that's what you're talking about. I don't think there's a quick and simple answer; it's not a yes or no. We live in the middle of a society where all these things happen. If you disallow them from having them, all their friends have them and they're going to get to play with them anyway. You've just dodged the issue; in effect, you've just dodged being with them where they have to struggle and survive. They need to talk about them. Any time something is very important to them, not just to young ones but to us, when we get fixed on something, we need to be a little suspicious. We need to have a chance to look at that, talk about it, see what sort of distress there is in that particular area, and work on it so we get a chance to think about it more flexibly.

I don't think that there's anything horribly wrong with the games that get played. People do get lost in some of them, but to make a decision from the outside that they can't do anything in that area, I think is a mistake. I think

I would let it go. Any time you have a suspicion of difficulty, what you can do is add your attention as counselor. Rather than going in there making decisions for them, get everybody talking about it; if the activity seems incorrect to you, don't just say no. Find a better solution, something else to do instead of that, that heads in the direction they want to go without the distresses connected with it.

On most of the questions that come to our minds about young ones, we can't decide them from the outside, we can't look down and say "They shouldn't do this" as if we know what is really going on. We have to go in awarely enough to make a relationship, so we can really find out what's going on. No young one wants to stay stubborn in their distresses any more than you do. Given the resource, supportive friendly resource, they'll figure a way to get out of wherever they're stuck.

ROCK CONCERTS

Question:

What is your opinion of rock concerts?

Tim:

Rock concerts. You don't like rock concerts? I'm always immediately suspicious of the standard terrors of adults that get put on newspaper pages, that rock concerts have got harmful, destructive tendencies. I don't see them as horrible things. They don't interest me greatly, either; but that isn't the question. The question is, is somebody stuck in distress, and how can you help them get free enough to make their decision? Rather than how do we decide it for them, it's how can they decide it themselves.

EARLY MEMORIES

Question:

Have you had any experience with very young children just learning to talk, talking about their birth?

Tim:

No. By and large, most of the young ones I've been with don't talk about the past very much. Sometimes it comes up or looks like it comes up when they play fantasies, but most young ones seem to be interested in present-day and future things, not going back there. That, in my mind, is related to the same question of why sessions with young people look so different. It is as if, for a while, the main task is collecting information about the world and learning enough. Only when you've acquired that certain set of information does it make sense to look back. But I haven't seen that happen at all, no.

SEX

Question:

There was a time when my daughter was interested in things like models, but the way she was interested was creepy, as if she couldn't think at all. . . I have watched TV with her and basically approved of what she was watching. Take "Charlie's Angels." I'm just embarrassed. In some ways I liked it. That was real good for a while. It seemed she wanted to decide for herself whether they were creeps, and not have her parents say, "We already know what this means." For a long time now, she has been reading novels about boys and girls that I didn't read when I was her age. I read some cats and horses books. It was easy for me to help her where the books were strange, because I was genuinely interested. I read every one she read, right behind her, faster. All this neat stuff that I didn't look at at all when I was her age — I was much too embarrassed. I loved it. The boy meets the girl, etc. But now, she's getting a little older and. . .

Tim:

Have you all got a picture in your mind where this is going?! (laughter)

Questioner:

It's going from Dick and Jane. . . Now I see the books and I think, "Oh, God, she shouldn't be reading this!"

and then I think, "Oh, I shouldn't be reading this!" I skip through the parts where they take off their clothes, and I come back and I don't know what to say to her.

Tim:

You want me to tell you what to say?! (laughter, more and more)

Questioner adds more details.

Tim:

Well, there aren't many good ways to get access to information about sex and sexual relations. (more laughing)

Questioner:

What I want to tell her is that sex is not weird, that actually women can have sex and have a whole lot of fun, but... I'd like her to know that I am sure that it's not true that women don't like sex, that women only have sex because of some weird aberration. I want to tell her that I know it's true, that someone can like sex for good reasons. It can be real nice. You know what I mean?

Tim:

Can you find books? She can't find books that say that. She's hunting for information, and the fact that there's a lot of distress in those books may not be the thing that attracts her at all. She's hunting for a way to understand sex, and having nobody she can talk to to get information and no book that makes any sense at all, she's trying to pick crumbs out of the other garbage in these books. I wouldn't worry about those books; they're not the problem. They're a symptom of the problem. The problem is, how can we find a way to get ourselves through enough of our distresses in this area that we can provide that information, either by writing the books or by being able to talk about things in ways that enough people can listen to us. That's where you want to put your effort, not worrying about those books particularly, but finding a way that you can try to talk with her, maybe after a lot of sessions trying to tell *your* best counselor all about sex — your rational attitude toward sex.

She doesn't have anyone better than you as a source of information. She really does not. She's very lucky to have you. You're a much better source than most people ever get. You mustn't put yourself down because you've got distress around it. Every other source she's got is much worse, much more heavily distressed than you are. You have to go ahead and try to do it. Maybe you have to write a story because you can't talk about it, and maybe you can find better sources than she's got — there are better sources than she's got, probably; (there aren't a lot of them) — but she needs your help in that, I think. I think it also helps to talk about how distressed those particular stories are, so she won't get confused by them.

It's all right, too, that you let all your embarrassment show. You won't fool her by keeping it down. You don't have to try to look prim and proper when you talk about sex. That won't help. It didn't help us, it won't help her. What she needs is you; she knows you and she knows that embarrrassment. It's all right that that's there; that won't confuse her at all. What she needs is you there, and you'll be more there letting that embarrassment run off than trying to hold it tightly in place.

WHEN TO STEP IN

Question:

Should an adult intervene in a situation where an adult is hitting a child?

Tim:

Yes, I think it's wise to step in. I think it's wise even if you bungle it. It's important for you to not give in to your timidities about it, your feelings of "Who are you to have an opinion?" You know it's incorrect. It's all right if you take a stand on it. It's important for the child, even though he or she never sees you again. Somebody knew it was wrong and did something about it. They only see you for that ten seconds; it still makes a difference to have some glimpse of the way the world could be outside of that family pattern of hitting the child. It's important. I know lots of people as adults who, in their counseling, go back to those little bits of memories. There was a day once when somebody reached in and made a difference. That inkling that it didn't have to be this way stayed alive because people did that. I think it's very important for both you and the young one, and it can be important for the adult. That adult does not want to hit the child, would give anything they could to not do that. He or she cannot think of anything else at that moment, in fact is not thinking at all. The person is frozen in distress. I think it's important you do something even if you bungle it, even if you just go up and grab a hand and say, "You're not going to do that here while I'm here." Straight threat. It's better than nothing. But I think there are lots better ways to do it. Let me go on from here.

You can always go up to that adult as an ally. The reason they're doing that is because they've gotten so restimulated they've lost track — it means they're feeling miserable, and will feel miserable later about having done that, if they ever get functional enough again to feel this way. (Some people don't. If it's gotten that tight, it's tight all the time, and they can't tell.) You can go in and take part of the load off them. You can see the situation developing. The young one is tired and cranky and in the shopping cart and mother has to get the shopping done and is under all these pressures with all the things she has to get done. There's no reason to blame mother for snapping or running out of slack, but there is something you can do about the situation. You can go in and say, "Looks like it's getting kind of hard. Is there something I can do for a little bit?" Easy enough to do. "I'll run him around in the cart if you want to get another cart and fill it up with what you need." Something like that. Maybe she won't be able to. Maybe you'll scare her. You never know what you're going to run into. But the times that I've done it and the times I've had it reported to me it's consistently helped the parent get a better perspective, and sort of step back and see there's someone else in the world. It isn't this tight, little, narrow battle that it felt like at that moment. Often it will prop the young one up.

What I do with young ones in supermarkets is, I smile. They're sitting there, they look back, and the fact that somebody's over there looking at them with a grin on his face will pull them out of all sorts of distress. You can do this in cars, you know, young ones in the back seat of the car for the twelfth hour; you're driving along, and they're about ready to go crazy back there, and you can flirt with them, a quick little flirt out the side window. It's a way of putting attention to them. You're not able to let them discharge and get some distress off and function better, but you can provide the resource to get their attention out of what was pulling at them. There's a skill that you develop as you practice with this ability. It's surprising what you can get away with. You can pull miserable-looking people out to fairly good functioning in a short while if you play it right, but you must remember you're aiming at pulling the attention out, not counseling them to discharge on their distress. You have a certain goal in mind in that situation in the middle of the department store, or whatever, and that is to get them out where they can function, to free some of their attention from their distress. You can always move in to try those things, even when you get rebuffed, or when it looks like they didn't notice it. It usually makes a difference anyway, and they just can't let you know that. I would always go ahead and try it if you have any slack at all. Usually if you're functioning well enough to see it, you've got enough slack that you can do something about it.

SEIZURES

Question:

How do you counsel someone who has a seizure during a counseling session?

Tim:

What do the seizures look like?

Questioner adds information.

Tim:

Well, like most important things, you never know for sure, especially ahead of time. You want to check and make sure there aren't physical difficulties, and you need to get as much information as you can. Find the best people who know as much as there is to be known, to check it out. You also want to consider the possibility that it's a distress coming up. If you see some similarity in the situations in which it happens, then it would be my suspicion that it's a distress pattern. I've known people who have seizures like that, and as near as I can tell, it was an attempt to work on very early, heavy distress that happened to them. The seizure itself never seemed to harm them. If people didn't panic around them and stayed warm and supportive and held them and let them be as scared as they wanted, they would shake for a long, long time and be in excellent shape the next day. So what I would say is just that. Check out all the physical things you can. You don't want to say you can cure anything with discharge. There aren't good grounds to say that, too many broken arms and things around. But there is a good possibility, with symptoms like that, that it does come from earlier distresses, and you can test it, having checked out everything else.

Most people get trapped into trying to suppress the symptoms of it, giving them a drug so that the symptoms don't show. Instead, let them show you that distress, be warm, supportive, reassuring. You have to play some hunches, or at least I do in that situation, of where the distress came from. Try to contradict your best picture of that distress. I often say something like, "I know it was hard back there, but you made it through that, and that's never going to happen again. I'm here with you now and you're safe. Safe enough for you to be as scared as you want." I try to figure out what it was, my best hunch, and contradict that. If I'm close to accurate, shaking increases usually. If I'm not very close, then things go on in spite of me. In my experience, when that resource is made available, the seizures will happen for a while, and then they subside. I've never had a situation where we ever got to know very much about what really happened.

You play your best cards and take your winnings, essentially, and never get to know. That's one of the hardest things about working with very young ones, especially when they can't talk yet. It's that you never know what they're working on for sure. You have your hunches, but it's not like your adult Co-Counselor who says, "I need to work on. . ." and tells you all about what happened. The young one may just act intransigent to you, or get upset or cranky, but is trying to work on something. In a real sense, it doesn't matter if you ever know. You can be a little more skillful in counseling sometimes if you have the information, but you can be a good enough counselor knowing nothing except that they're working on "something." That's enough to go ahead.

FEELINGS TOWARD AN UNBORN CHILD

Question:

I have negative feelings toward the child I am pregnant with. Should I counsel on it?

Tim:

Well, you *do* have that distress. If you've got it, you have it. Your keeping quiet about it probably doesn't shield the child. The rest of us may not notice, we're so used to things like that. My general guideline has always been that if you can find a way to work on it effectively, it's better than leaving it and not working on it. I think you have to take some care in counseling on it. It's best not to allow yourself to play out the feelings, to get lost in feeling the distress, but rather, work on contradicting the distress. The tone of your counseling is probably more important here because there's somebody that closely involved. I would work on it right from the beginning by contradiction rather than by saying how bad it is, or by questioning the distress rather than by showing the distress. I would work on it. I don't think there's a reason not to. There's a reason to be thoughtful about it.

MASTURBATION

Question:

My child masturbates a lot. What should I do?

(Much laughter)

Tim:

Well, you have to face the fact that there is something interesting there. There is a reason to be interested and to experiment. That's not a problem. Unfortunately, in this society there is such a heavy load of distress around that area, that most of us pick up distresses around that area and it freezes us into compulsive behavior, where we're not really finding anything out any more. It's locked up in distresses and fantasies in our heads. Those distresses are a problem. The particular symptom of it, of masturbation, probably isn't. You don't want to get worried about that symptom because it upsets everybody you know. (laughter) It's only an indication of how something got frozen on this person, something that they need to work on. The thing itself is just a silly little symptom that happens to upset everybody. It's not important. The distress in there that has been locked in that way, that's important. I wouldn't worry about suppressing that symptom unless it gets played out in a way that makes them a target for attacks consistently. Then maybe short-range, you have to find a way to hide the symptom, but that's a very short-range tactical consideration. The distress is what needs your attention; that's where the help needs to go.

REALITY, DEATH

Question:

(something quite general about life and death)

Tim:

Living, death, reality; it's getting a little fuzzy. (laughter)

Just the way you were talking about it reminds me of an important point that escapes people a lot, about the role you can have with young ones. There are a lot of things you can do as a counselor for young ones, whether or not you're a parent. Non-parents play a very important role in setting up relationships with young ones. Finding a young one and committing yourself internally, making a commitment to yourself to spend an hour with that young one every week and arranging it so they can count on it, makes a very big difference for a young one. It changes their picture of life. They get to go out and do things with you they can't do with their folks. They get to go play pinball machines if their folks can't stand that. They get to eat at Burger King, or wherever.

They get to try things that their family distresses keep them from experimenting with. For a lot of parents it's useful to have that kind of deal. You have no idea how useful it is until you start doing it. It will be useful in your life, for your perspective about what life is, and it will be excellent for your counseling. It will open up areas for you to counsel on that you haven't found a way to look at before. It'll give you a new perspective.

As well as being a counselor, there's something we can do with young people, and that is provide a picture of reality, an understanding of reality. That's one of the things counseling has given us. It gives us a way to understand why things are happening. The world is tough to make some sense of unless you have a good model of it, and counseling is probably one of the best that you'll ever find. To try to help a young one understand why things happen around them, all the strange things that happen, to give them some way of understanding why they happen and to be able to predict other things happening off that model, is a very big step for them. To know there's a way to understand all these things, a way to make sense of it, that it all fits together, that there's a way to keep it all in one package and not just all scattered, is very useful for a young one. You can always do that. Until they get the information to set up their own picture of the world fully, they need to rely on yours, and you need to give them the best, clearest way of understanding that you can. That's the job that you need to do actively.

Death is interesting, too. I mean it really is interesting Most of us never got a chance to find out about it or think about it or talk about it, because everyone else was scared. So somebody died and what did they tell you? They're gone. And if they looked sad enough you never asked them the question: Where? "They went to sleep." What happened to my dog? "They put him to sleep." All of these strange little phrases that don't give anyone any information about what actually happened. Death is interesting. Something is actually going on there. Any real phenomenon is interesting. It's all right to be interested in it, to try to find out about it and know about it and understand it. Children try to find out about everything, no matter how your distresses lie. They want to know about everything, until they run into you anyway.

What I've seen work is to experiment with death, for young ones to have that chance. Carefully controlling the experiment! Plants that don't get watered. How long can you let them go and water them again and have them come back? And when do they pass that point? (laughter) A number of families down in my area have pets for their children, and they make sure that at least some of the pets are short-lived. A rat doesn't live a very long life. I mean, its life-span is not long. They get to watch the rat age and die. I've gone over to my Co-Counselor's house and this little white rat will be sitting there trembling on the sofa. It's getting near time, you know. Then, after the pet dies, they bury it in the back yard and put a marker over it. They dig it up every couple of days, to watch what happens, to see what goes on, to try to get some understanding of what's actually happening. That seems to make a lot of sense. You can talk about it and you can try to give good information about it, but to actually see, actually see what happens to a living creature when it dies and what happens afterwards, answers a lot of questions that you will find awkward, if not impossible.

You can give some picture of the physical processes that are operating, that we call life, and the fact that something happens to stop them from operating and that that lump of matter no longer functions the way it used to, that it stops and it's not recoverable. The question always edges in on human death, and, "Are you going to die, Mommy?" That's the one that always puzzles adults a lot. You can give information on it, and that's part of what's being asked for, but the question about whether, "Are you going to die, Mommy?" is more, in my experience, "Are you going to give up?" That's really what's being asked a lot. Are you going to give up and die? The best answer I've come up with (I can't argue with the fact that I haven't known anyone who has survived past a certain number of years) but what I can say is that I don't intend to. I may, I may not figure it out, I may get killed, it may even make sense in a strugglc that that happens, but it is never my intention. There's some sort of reassurance in that.

Other Publications by Rational Island Publishers on Relations with Young People

The Caring Parent, journal for people interested in parenting. Issues No. 1 and 2 available, $2.00 each; Issue No. 4 available, $3.00 each.

Young and Powerful, journal for young people and everyone interested in young people. Issue No. 4 available, $2.00 each.

Classroom, a journal of the theory and practice of learning and educational change. Issues No. 1 and 2 available, $1.00 each; Issues No. 3, 4, 5, and 8 available, $2.00 each.

Permit Their Flourishing, pamphlet, by the staff of Palo Alto Pre-school. Description of the first year of the pre-school. ISBN 0-911214-59-3. $2.00.

How to Give Children an Emotional Headstart, pamphlet, by Marion Riekerk. Illustrated, succinct tenets for interacting with young people. ISBN 0-913937-33-9. $1.00.